P9-BZJ-406

THE METTLACH BOOK

ILLUSTRATED CATALOG
CURRENT PRICES
COLLECTOR'S INFORMATION

BY
GARY KIRSNER

EDITOR
JIM GRUHL

SEVEN HILLS BOOKS, CINCINNATI, OHIO

While every care has been taken in the compiling of information contained in this volume neither the author nor the publisher can accept any liability for loss, financial or otherwise, incurred by reliance placed on the information herein.

©MCMLXXXIII Gary Kirsner

All rights reserved. No part of this book may be reproduced or utilized in any form or by any means, electronic or mechanical, including photocopying, recording, or by any information storage and retrieval system, without permission in writing from the author.

Library of Congress Cataloging in Publication Data

Kirsner, Gary, 1945 -
   The Mettlach book.

   Bibliography: p. 297
   Includes index.
   1. Villeroy & Boch. 2. Pottery, German. 3. Pottery—19th century—German (West) 4. Pottery—20th century—Germany (West) I. Gruhl, Jim. II. Title.
NK4210.V48K57 1983   738.2'3   82-62880
ISBN 0-911403-18-3

Printed in the United States of America
Published by Seven Hills Books
519 West Third Street
Cincinnati, OH 45202
Telephone (513) 381-3881

CONTENTS

Cover Photo: Stein 2778 1.0L

Preface

Several stein collectors have recently heard that I was writing this book and including the "real" Mettlach prices. The same questions came from many of them, "Why would you want to tell everybody about the steins that a few advanced collectors and dealers know are worth three or four times the price listed in the available price guides? Won't this be bad for your stein business?" The answer is that I don't want to see the hobby begin to slip under the control of those who have this *inside information;* this would breed mistrust, suspicion, and disappointment among the majority of collectors. So, I think it will be unquestionably good for the hobby, and therefore good for dealers like me, to have the "real" prices be known by all; this fosters trust, openness, and enthusiasm.

Again it is this interest, admittedly vested, that has led me away from a mimeographed price list and toward a book with much information and many pictures that will contribute to the growing and thriving of Mettlach collecting. In addition to questions about prices there have been scores of excellent Mettlach questions that I have been asked by collectors:

- how were these wares made?
- what effect does condition have on what collectors will pay?
- which steins or plaques are in certain sets?
- what do some of the really rare pieces look like?
- when were the different trademarks used?
- how many steins did Mettlach make?

Aside from scattered and unpublished results of research there has been no place that collectors could find the answers. This is the material that is presented in this book; and it is the collectors who deserve the credit, for they have asked the excellent questions and for the most part they have done the research. My task then has been one of a compiler of this scattered information, and I believe that there is much in this book that will be new and exciting to both beginning and advanced collectors. I would *very much* appreciate a letter or call if you have other questions or suggestions about what might be included in possible future editions.

I have occasionally been asked personal questions and although I am somewhat reluctant to include the answers in this book, the editor insisted. I studied economics and accounting at New York University and Miami University of Ohio. I began dealing in antiques in the early 1970's and concentrated exclusively on steins and Mettlach wares shortly thereafter. Thanks to a great number of collectors, I found it was not only possible to deal solely in steins and other Mettlach wares, but I was fortunate to soon become the leading dealer of quality steins. For some time I carried an inventory of almost nothing but Mettlach; it is now about two-thirds of my business, with the remainder primarily character steins, regimental steins, and 17th and 18th Century steins. I have an additional hobby of restoring old German sports cars. I now live in a small restored house in Glenford, upstate New York, with my wife Karen and daughters Beth and Britt, a family I enjoy tremendously.

I appreciate that all of the research, writing, traveling, photographing, and layout of this book, on top of my full-time stein dealing, required substantial sacrifices by my family. However, they not only tolerated this situation, but cheerfully supported it with typing, sorting, and other time consuming tasks. There are a number of other people I would specifically like to thank for their help, information, hospitality, and because they are some of the same people who make being part of the stein community such a very pleasant experience: Andre Ammelounx, Hans Ammelounx, Wally Andrews, Jack Cooper, John Crowley, Jim DeMars, Joe Durban, Mark Durban, Steve Elliot, Ron Fox, Ron Garlick, Bernie Gould, Jim Hansen, Aurel Keck, Frank Love, Phil Mislivec, Harvey Murphy, Gordon Nicklos, Jack Pandl, Les Paul, Mel Preszler, and those who wish to remain anonymous. In this group also belong Jim Gruhl, Richard Jones and Bob Wilson, but I would like as well to give them *special* thanks for their generous assistance at several stages in this project.

My hope is that this book will help people to find that Mettlach collecting is not just a hobby, it is beauty, excitement, and history, and it tells us something very wonderful about the previous generations and about ourselves.

Gary Kirsner
Glentiques, Ltd.
P.O. Box 337
Glenford, N.Y. 12433
(914) 657-6261

1. Mettlach History and Trademarks

First it should be noted that a great number of scholarly researchers have worked diligently to uncover facts about Mettlach wares. The bibliography in section 11 lists a number of these scholars' dissertations which are available for those with a desire for detailed information. Presented here is just a scratching of the surface of this deep and fascinating area of knowledge.

1.1 History

It seems worth a few paragraphs at the outset to recount the manner in which the paths of politics, technology, art, marketing, and the economics and skills of the labor force happened to cross in just such a manner as to result in the creation of a product so aesthetic and irreproducible that it has become one of the premier antique collectables.

Mettlach, from the Latin word for *mid-lakes,* is a small village on the Saar River in what is now the far western part of West Germany, near both Luxembourg and France. Although the ceramic products made here were produced by the Villeroy and Boch Company, V&B, they have commonly been called *Mettlach* wares. Apparently this was done partly to avoid confusion with the very different products made at the eight V&B factories in other cities, and partly because the name Mettlach dominates the important incised *old tower* or *castle* trademark used by the Mettlach factory.

Pierre-Joseph Boch, the founder of the family pottery business, had a son Jean Francis Boch who studied chemistry and mineralogy at the Ecole des Sciences in Paris. After Jean Francis completed his studies he began searching for a place to begin a pottery so he could make use of his education. Utilizing the fortunes of his family and of his wife, Rosalie Buschmann, in 1809 he purchased for their Boch-Buschmann firm the old Benedictine Abbey of Mettlach, including its expansive central buildings and its famous old tower. The abbey was founded late in the 7th Century; the tower was constructed from the years

987 to 1000, modeled after a cathedral built by Charlemagne in 786. Most of the central buildings were constructed in the mid-18th Century, but during the French Revolution the monks were driven out and the buildings confiscated by the French Republic. The Republic then sold the plundered and partially ruined buildings to Mr. Boch.

Flower Pot 1128

The choice of the Mettlach site presented many advantages and disadvantages that all played important roles in the development of the products that were to come from this factory. The advantages were obvious: minimal competition within this political and tariff-free region, fine raw materials, a navigable Saar River, and idyllically beautiful surroundings. There were two major disadvantages. First, although some workers from others of the Boch's factories were moved to Mettlach, the twenty families of fisherman that were then the extent of the Mettlach population hardly provided a thriving reserve of skilled laborers and artisans. Second, the government had imposed a condition on the sale of the buildings that the abundant hard coal resources, and not the scarce wood, must be used to fire the kilns. This presented a tremendous obstacle because it required the invention of a coal-burning kiln, which was only accomplished in 1816, but did result in a far superior and more uniform firing.

Flower Pot 1128, view of *Schloss Ziegelberg*

Mettlach innovations did not come solely through necessity. Water power was harnessed for turning the potters' wheels and for the clay preparation machinery. These novel labor-saving advances helped the enterprise cope with the skyrocketing wage demands of the new middle class that followed the French Revolution. Other advances came when the copper plate engraving and transfer printing techniques from Staffordshire England were brought to Met-

Flower Pot 1128, view of the *Monastery* and the back of the *Old Tower*

tlach in 1820, and excellent common wares were produced that appealed to the newly monied middle class. Art studios, archives, museums, art schools, and famous artists were all brought to Mettlach in an effort to further promote the artistic accomplishments of the factory.

With the business then in the hands of Jean Francis' son Eugene, in 1836 a merger with Nicholas Villeroy's factory was undertaken in order to eliminate the only significant competition that had arisen in the region. This created the Villeroy and Boch Company. Soon after this there was a loosening of the hold of the Empire and Biedermeier styles that demanded only mundane wares, and Mettlach found a market for the decorative relief beakers and steins, in the style of historicism, which they then produced in great numbers.

Also at this time August von Cohausen, a historian, architect, archaeologist, and friend of Eugene Boch, was hired as Deputy Director of the Mettlach facility. Cohausen's training had conditioned him to revere the past, and he had a strong influence on the achievements that followed. He instigated the restoration of the old abbey tower and the use of it as a factory trademark. He also supported the building of a railroad which was opened along the Saar River in 1860 and substantially improved transportation: of raw materials, of finished articles, and of a workforce that could now expand comfortably along the river valley. In 1878 and 1879 Cohausen pushed strongly for the "fabrication of stoneware in the spirit of the Renaissance...it is not necessary that the antique must be slavishly imitated, however one must imitate the production methods of that time."

Close-up of shield on 1723 .5L, VB is for Villeroy and Boch, stein pictured has an EB on shield for Eugene Boch.

1723 .5L Town of Mettlach

1723 .5L Inlay, *Old Tower*

Silver medal presented to employees for 25 years of service.

The golden age of Mettlach began shortly thereafter and lasted approximately from 1880 to 1910, during which, using guarded secret techniques, the etched, glazed, cameo, and phanolith wares were at the pinnacle of their productions. New design lines and an explosion of color were then brought into the production of the Mettlach items. An extensive display at the 1885 Antwerp World's Fair propelled Mettlach into the forefront of the ceramics field, with reviewers using descriptions such as *Vollkommenes* = perfection, and *geradezu unerreicht* = frankly unrivalled. Production quantities continued to grow until at its height the Mettlach plant employed about 1250 people. For example, in June 1898 there were 1251 factory employees, 130 were working in the printing shop, 47 at lithography, 36 at the painting of Delft styles and earthenware, and 89 at the painting of stoneware.

Especially during this golden age, V&B provided a high quality lifestyle for its employees. They had transportation, medical care, insurance, pensions, mortgages, schools, co-op stores, restaurants, parks with lakes and extensive gardens, and entertainment including band concerts, picnics, bowling, billiards, a gymnasium, library, theater, and bath house, all in a beautiful and romantic setting. By all accounts the factory and other employees, which numbered about 2500 (Thieler, 1909), had almost legendary loyalty to the firm, and keeping the techniques of production secret presented no problem.

About 1909, and certainly by the time of the First World War, business seems to have slacked off considerably. Researchers of this subject tend to blame unfavorable economic circumstances and a lack of skilled labor. In 1921 a great fire destroyed all the molds, production records, and formulas for the production processes and materials, including the 30 colored clay slips, 150 under-glaze colors, and 176 colored hard glazes. From 1925 until the early 1930's some few etched and PUG articles were again being produced at the Mettlach plant.

Although the Mettlach factory continued to produce tiles, dishes, plumbing fix-tures, and other wares, there was almost a fifty year lapse before they recently revived the stein and plaque manufacturing. Although some of the most desirable steins and plaques have been reproduced, the processes and materials were obviously different. The quality of these reproduced pieces is admirable but they are so noticeably inferior to the original chromolith items that most collectors would rather have comparably priced antique PUGs.

Shapespeare writes in *The Tempest* that "What's past is prologue." How can this prologue of past Mettlach history tell us what now is in store for the future? It is true that the secret formulas, labor-intensive technologies, and socio-economic situations that resulted in the production of the Mettlach wares are irretrievable. Thus, these *"frankly unrivalled"* wares are almost certainly going to remain so. It is a sad circumstance but it does inspire confidence in the collector who goes to some expense to obtain the irreproducible quality and beauty of these antique Mettlach articles.

As for the future of Mettlach prices, the collector is not now the only force shaping the market, because major museums have just begun to gather collec-tions. In the past, museums were apparently somewhat reluctant to introduce *mass-produced* art into their permanent collections, even though they did own Rembrandt and Picasso multiples that were more common than the rarer Met-tlachs. In the late 1970's some museums tested the level of public appreciation for Mettlach wares with some exhibits. These were tremendously successful, and boosted both the public's and the museums' desires to begin collections. These collections have been started at several major museums in the United States and abroad, such as those at Hamburg, Munich, Bonn, Sevres, Amsterdam, Zurich, and others. Some have budgeted substantial funds for these quests. This bodes well for the investment potential of fine Mettlach wares and bodes poorly for the chances of future generations of collectors.

1.2 Trademarks

With the Mettlach trademarks, as with those of many other factories, there were enough variations to allow a determination of the approximate year of production merely by an examination of the mark. This is particularly impor-tant for dating items from the early Mettlach period, before the year of produc-tion began to be coded onto the pieces.

The bottom or back of almost every Mettlach product has a trademark. Those few that are occasionally found not to be marked seem to frequently be

PUGs from about 1900 or later or relief wares from around 1860. These may once have had marks: occasionally stamped trademarks are found nearly worn off because some were put *over* the glaze; some of the applied trademarks have been found glued back on or partially broken off.

The majority of the Mettlach items on the market will have some form of the *old tower,* or so-called *castle,* mark, see Fig. 1. Actually this is a representation of the old abbey church that was completed in the year 1000. This trademark was first used in about 1883, and has been revived for use on the currently produced Mettlach articles where it is encircled by an incised *METTLACH COLLECTORS SOCIETY.* By far the most common of these tower marks was the 1885-1930 version with the incised *banner,* which is actually two separate marks, the tower and the banner. One particularly astute Mettlach researcher has catalogued the apparently contrived variations in the lettering and shapes of the banner portion of this mark (which become more contrived in later years) and has made a convincing argument that this was the scheme used by the factory for identifying the work of individual potters!

Another very common trademark is the so-called *Mercury* mark, see Fig. 2. This design consists of the winged head of Mercury, the god of commerce, with two snake-entwined staffs over *Villeroy & Boch* in a strapwork banner. Below the banner are two or four semi circles with the name *Mettlach,* and scalloping with between 10 and 13 dots - dots which will later be shown to be important in one dating system. All of the V&B factories used this type of trademark, of course with their respective city name. None of the products of these other factories are listed in this book.

There are some additional names and words that are found on some Mercury marks. Dinnerware pattern names, such as *ELLA, LOTTE,* and *ADELE,* can be seen inside the semicircles. Declarations of copyright protections (in the U.S. it is common to see *Reg. U.S. Pat. Off.*) sometimes occur below the scalloping, and these are described in the next subsection. Some Mercury stamps were not protected by the usual hard clear glaze and can thus be found at various stages of wear.

Many of the early and other unusual Mettlach trademarks are displayed in Figs. 3, 4, and 5. They require little explanation. Recall that when the Mettlach pottery was founded in 1809 it was named after the two families who provided the investment capital, Boch and Buschmann. The earliest marks were generally incised and carried this name, as shown at the top of Fig. 3. The 1836 merger with Villeroy naturally started a whole new progression of trademarks, generally using the initials V B, although the mark with the incised full name *Villeroy & Boch* is perhaps the most common early trademark. Porcelain, PUG, faience, and Delft wares mostly carry glazed-over stamped or hand-painted trademarks. Etched, relief, cameo, and later PUG, items generally have incised marks, and sometimes stamped trademarks as well.

1883
incised tower with
applied banner

1883-c.1886
incised

1885-c.1930
incised

1906-1910
incised

1925-1931
green stamped

1930's
blue stamped

Fig. 1 Approximate dates of use for some of the various *Old Tower* trademarks found on many etched, relief, cameo, and other Mettlach wares.

Fig. 2 These are a few of the 30 or so variations of the Mercury trademark. It was used from 1874 to about 1909 on PUG and other wares, always being stamped on, generally in green but sometimes in blue, black, or brown.

ℬ:ℬ:

1810-c.1813 incised
or blue mark

Boch Buschmann a Mettlach
I.

c.1813-1825
incised

c.1820-1845
incised

Mettlacher Hartsteingut

c.1830-1850
incised

Bochet Buschmann a Mettlach

c.1813-1825
incised

Villeroy & Boch.

1836-1855
incised

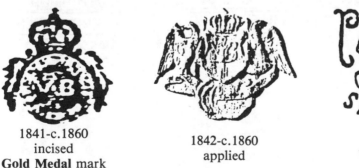

1841-c.1860
incised
Gold Medal mark

1842-c.1860
applied

1844-c.1860
blue stamped

Fig. 3 The earliest *Mettlach* trademarks and the very approximate years they were utilized.

1844-c.1870
violet or blue stamped
Gold Medal mark

c.1850's
incised

c.1852-1873
applied with form number
incised in center, often
just with form number

c.1855-1876
blue or black
stamped

c.1860's
stamped

c.1860-1874
blue stamped

c.1870
gold stamped

1873-1883
applied

Fig. 4 Some trademarks used during the important developmental period, along with very approximate years of use.

c.1880-1883
applied

c.1880's
black or brown
stamped

c.1880-1883
incised

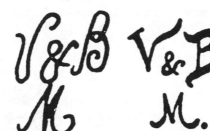

all these are c.1890-1910
blue stamped or painted

c.1885-1895
incised

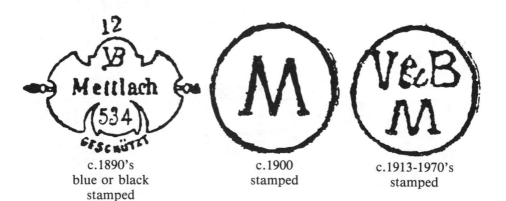

c.1890's
blue or black
stamped

c.1900
stamped

c.1913-1970's
stamped

Fig. 5 Miscellaneous trademarks from the most productive Mettlach period, the *decoration number* was occasionally incorporated into the stamped trademarks as can be seen with *601* in the strapwork stamp and the *534* in the shield.

1.3 Mettlach Marking Systems

Fortunately, throughout the important Mettlach period from about 1880 to 1910 the factory marked their products consistently and profusely, see Fig. 6. Of course some of these marks are of little importance to collectors because they were intended for the identification of individual craftsmen and for quality control purposes. However, many of the marks *are* interesting to collectors and these are the ones described here.

A most important mark is the one that shows the *form* number, sometimes called the *mold* or *stock* number; it is the large Arabic number impressed into the base or back of Mettlach wares. This is generally a three- or four-digit number and is usually located below the trademark. Even when the trademark is not present the distinctive crisp style of the form number, see Fig. 6, can be used, together with an examination of quality, to identify Mettlach items.

A *decoration* number was used for identifying the design on PUG, Rookwood, and some faience products. This number was stamped on PUGs and Rookwoods, and painted on faiences, usually in black or blue, and generally occurred with *Geschutzt* (patented) or *DEC.* (abbreviation for *Dekoration?*).

The exact year of production can often be discerned from the marks on an item. The earliest dating system was used in conjunction with the block-lettered VILLEROY & BOCH shown in Fig. 4. The years 1861 to 1870 were represented respectively by 1 to 10 dots starting under the left side of the name; 1 to 6 dots starting under the right side denote 1871 to 1876.

A dot-dating system was also sometimes used with the Mercury marks. If there are more than 10 dots under the scalloping at the bottom of a Mercury mark, or if a copyright notice or other writing takes the usual place of the dots, then that mark has no date code. If there are 13 scallops at the bottom of the Mercury mark, and some of the dots are missing, then the number of dots left should be added to 1870 to find the year of production. If the scalloping is also missing wherever there are missing dots, then 1 to 9 dots, starting from the right, represent 1881 to 1889 respectively. If the 10-scalloped pattern is used and it goes the complete length of the semicircle, then the years 1891 to 1899 are represented respectively by 1 to 9 dots starting from the right, and the years 1901 to 1909 are represented by 1 to 9 dots starting usually from the left (but occasionally, ambiguously, from the right). Years 1890 and 1900 both have the full compliment of 10 dots and are thus indistinguishable; there was no Mercury mark used in 1910.

The most important date code is the two-digit incised number that often is located to the right and below the trademark, as can be seen in Fig. 6. Items made from 1882 to 1887 have an 82 to 87 incised inside a small rectangle. For 1888 and after the rectangle was not used, so for example 88 is 1888, 95 is 1895, 00 is 1900, 05 is 1905, and so on.

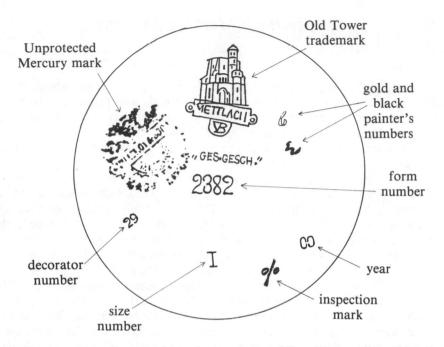

Fig. 6 Bottom of a well-marked Mettlach stein: a 1.0 liter 2382 made in 1900, the MADE IN GERMANY barely visible around the bottom of the Mercury mark indicated that this stein was probably exported.

It seems that an etched Mettlach item made long after the initial production year is an indication both that (1) the etching may be slightly inferior to previous examples, and (2) the longevity probably indicates that this was one of the more popular products. It can thus be desirable to know the initial production year for an item that is being examined for potential purchase. Robert D. Wilson has developed an *accurate* graph, shown in (Wilson, Sept. 1979), that connects form numbers to their first year of production. Here is an *approximate* formula for initial dating of V&B form numbers that are between 1200 and 3200. Begin by taking one hundreth of the form number, call this **Y**. Add Y + ⅓Y + 65 and the result approximates the initial production year. For example, for V&B 2100, 21 + 7 + 65 = 93, that is to say 1893. For V&B 3089, a little rounding will not hurt so 31 + 10 + 65 = 106 or 1906. The average error between these mentally calculable dates and those in the Wilson graph is about a quarter of a year.

Establishing the first year of production for items with decoration numbers is less important, but (Decoration Number)/30 + 65 will give a fair approximation for decoration numbers between 600 and 1400. These formulas tell us that from about 1880 to 1910 the Mettlach factory was quite consistently turning out about 75 new forms and 30 new decorations annually.

As shown in Fig. 6, Mettlach items can often be found with hand-painted gold, black, or other colored numbers, letters, or symbols on the base. These were the identification marks of the craftsmen responsible for the gold work, the glazing or highlight painting, or other hand decorations on the article.

An incised one- or two-digit *mystery* number is generally located to the left and below the trademark. This number is usually between 1 and 40 but can be as high as 57. It is certainly not the *week* of production as some used to believe. Most likely it is the number of the *principal decorator,* or perhaps the area in the factory where the item was produced.

Many Mettlach products have an additional large incised number under the mold number, usually a Roman numeral from I to V, but sometimes an Arabic numeral. Prior to 1899 this mark indicated how many different sizes existed with the same design. The largest size was denoted I, the second largest II, and so on; so, for example, a II didn't mean the same capacity for all form numbers! In 1899 this was changed and the following uniform system was initiated:

Size Number	Capacity in Liters
2/0 (only on PUG body 1526)	3.0
0 (only on PUG body 1526)	2.0
I	1.0
II	.5
III	.4
IV	.3
V	.25

On the PUG plaque 1044 the following size designation system was used:

Size Number	Plaque Diameter in Inches
2/0	22½''
0	19''
I	17½''
II	14''
III	12''
IV	10½''
V	8½''
VI	7½'' or 8''

In addition, the capacity of the steins was incised or hand painted on the side of most smaller steins, in the rear near the handle at the lip. Except for some early steins the sizes were regularly marked on the 1-liter and smaller steins. As a general rule the larger sizes of Mettlach steins were never marked with capacities.

There are any number of other incised or stamped marks that can occasionally be found on Mettlach wares; here are some common examples and their meanings:

GEGEN NACHBILDUNG GESCHUTZT, which means *against copying protected,* was incised and used in and before 1899,

GES. GESCH., an incised mark that is an abbreviation for *gesetzlich geschutzt* which means *legally protected,* and was used in and after 1899,

GESCHUTZT, meaning *protected* or *patented,* stamped or incised on a few articles,

MUSTERSCHUTZ, meaning *protected against copying,*

Made in Germany, or just *GERMANY,* stamped in green or incised, indicates the item was meant to be exported to the United States or elsewhere outside Germany, this mark was required after the 1891 *Marking Law,*

Reg. U.S. Pat. Off., registered U.S Patent Office, stamped, usually in green, on items intended for sale in the United States,

Made in Saar-Basin, used between 1918 and 1935 when Mettlach was in the French Protectorate initiated after World War I,

Echt Mettlach, meaning *genuine Mettlach,* and

Fabrik-Marke, meaning *factory mark,* occasionally stamped in conjunction with the trademark.

A green % mark can sometimes be found stamped under glaze on the bottom or back of Mettlach items, see Fig. 7. This is frequently mistaken for a *second* or *reject* mark, apparently because of the implication that a *percent* is less than whole or perfect. However, no correlation exists between the occurrence of this mark and noticeable factory flaws. In fact, items with this mark tend to be slightly *above* average in factory quality. Thus, this mark *appears* to be an indication that an item has *passed* an examination or sample testing that was conducted on a small, randomly selected, percentage of the articles produced (somewhere in the vicinity of five percent).

Before some new items were put into full-scale production, versions with varied body designs, different decorations, and/or different colors were produced. These samples were usually marked *Probe* or *P* meaning *trial* or *test-piece,* see Fig. 7. Apparently after the examination of one or more of these *probes* a desired version was selected and went into production. The probe mark occurs just by itself, or with any or all of the other marks normally found on Mettlach products, and was apparently only used after about 1885. Unique variations of earlier products have been seen but they simply carry the same form number as the version that was selected to go into production. The probes or early variations are rarely substantially different from the ultimate versions.

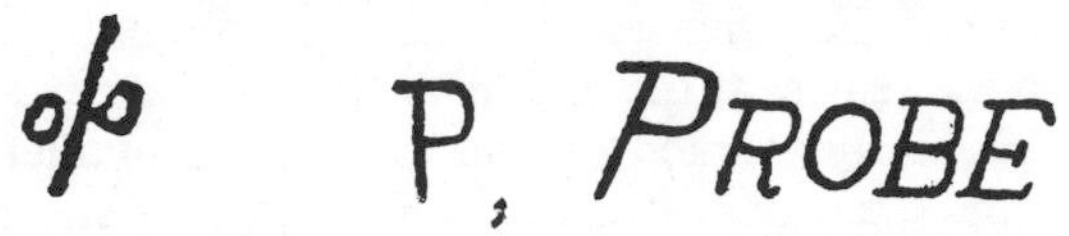

Fig. 7 The inspection and *Probe* marks.

2. Production of Mettlach Wares

The Villeroy and Boch Company produced steins and other wares that were, almost without exception, both original in design and in production technique. The exceptions include some plaques with designs replicating paintings of *old masters,* and a small number of steins that copied then-antique vessels such as Creussens, Annabergs, and faience.

Rarely, V&B steins were made and marked by Dresden, Luxembourg, or V&B factories other than the one at Mettlach. The majority of V&B steins, of course, were made at the Mettlach factory, and most all of these and the other wares they produced have certain common characteristics. Mettlach wares were made from a very hard impervious stoneware material which was homogeneous and vitrified. A pure white, porcelain-like glaze was applied to the insides of almost all drinking vessels and punch bowls. The primary exceptions are the steins marked BAVARIA which are a grey color inside and out. The same general type of stoneware that formed the bodies of the wares was also used in the decorations on the etched, relief, and mosaic items. Mold marks are generally not visible, indicating a very careful cleaning of the seams after the body was formed, or the use of potters' wheels to form or clean the bodies. An exceptional mold line is frequently visible on some steins made before about 1885 or after 1905. The handles were applied at a late stage in the production process, and it is clear that some bases were also applied.

2.1 Relief

The earliest steins produced at Mettlach were bas-relief in style, commonly called *relief.* The earliest decorations usually consisted of green or brown leaves and vines (Fig. 8) against brown or tan backgrounds. Occasionally the early relief pieces were accented with a platinum decoration. Eventually the designs used on these early wares evolved into figures (Fig. 9) and other more decorative relief scenes. Some experimentation with different colors also took place, and there are examples of some relief steins with decorations or backgrounds in three or more color variations, sometimes including a bisque white finish (Fig. 10). These earliest relief steins were produced from the 1840's through the early 1880's, when diversification into a variety of other production methods took place.

After about 1880 some of the early relief steins, such as form numbers 24, 202, and 485, were produced using the new highly refined production techniques (Fig. 11) invented at Mettlach. The design on the relief wares seems to have been produced in two ways. Rarely it appears that the relief has been applied by hand; the common method was apparently to form the design in a full-bodied mold. After an opaque tan relief material was set into the mold, a colored background stoneware-slip was painted into the mold, usually of a light blue, green, brown, grey, or coral red color. Single solid color relief steins are uncommon; these usually are all grey, brown, or bisque white.

It appears as if these steins were made in the style of the Siegburg stoneware. Several other stein manufacturers were also at that time producing similar, if not equally fine quality, grey relief steins. The Mettlach relief steins were among the least expensive steins they produced, and this is still true in today's market. The numbers used to identify the relief molds are primarily lower than 1000, with increasingly fewer molds numbered in the 1000's, 2000's, and 3000's.

Fig. 8 216 .5L

Fig. 9 202 1.0L
gnome on inlay

Fig. 10 485 .5L
bisque white

Fig. 11 24 .5L early style
and later refined style

2.2 Cameo and Phanolith

Cameo and relief wares are often confused with each other. Their production processes seem to be quite similar, except that (1) the cameos do not protrude as far from the body as the reliefs, thus calling for closer tolerances, and (2) the material used in the cameo reliefwork is a more translucent, porcelain-like material that allows for shadings of background colors to show through the thinnest portions of the relief. The resultant product (Fig. 12) is similar to the

gemstone and shell cameos, from which they get their name. The background color on most of the cameo wares is a light drab green; occasionally on later pieces a nice dark blue was used that tends to better show through the translucent decorations. There are some designs that were usually made in the cameo style that occasionally were produced with the opaque *relief*-type decoration, so direct examinations of items must be made to be certain that they are cameos. The cameo numbers are in the 2000's and 3000's, commencing in about 1893, about 50 years after the relief wares were first produced.

Why did it take about 50 years to discover a way to substitute a porcelain-like material for the opaque stoneware in the relief wares? The difficulty arose from the fact that porcelain shrinks as much as 20% more than stoneware when they are fired. Essentially the Mettlach craftsmen had to discover a new for-

Fig. 12 2754 .5L

Fig. 13 Plaque 7083

mula for a porcelain-like material with the same coefficient of reduction as the stoneware had, so as to avoid the firing separations that would otherwise occur between dissimilar materials.

Phanolith plaques (Fig. 13) and other objects (but no steins) were produced in the same monolithic molding process as the cameo. However, the materials used, and the tolerances of the process itself, may have been even finer in the phanolith than in the cameo. Phanolith wares were numbered exclusively in the 7000's and were produced principally between 1900 and 1908.

2.3 Print Under Glaze, Rookwood, Faience, and Delft

The simplest steins to produce were the *print under glaze* (Fig. 14), or *PUG* steins. A small number of blank forms were used for PUGs: various sizes of 1526 and 1909, as well as 2271 and 2140 ½-liters, were the most common stein blanks, and various sizes of 1044 were used for PUG plaques. After the blank body was formed, fired, and glazed, a decal-type or transfer printed scene was applied and the body was covered with an additional coat of transparent glaze, and refired. Actually the process could best be described as print between glazes. After the final firing the transfer scene had become an integral part of the product.

While most PUG wares are fairly simple in form, some of the punch bowls and a couple of steins were transfer decorated onto contoured surfaces. Some of the PUG steins, such as the 2271's and 2140's, have glazed body frieze bands similar to those found on most of the etched steins. Otherwise the PUG wares are quite consistently simple, and vary only slightly in quality of production. The color red, and sometimes the blue, will have different degrees of brightness, but on the whole only a small percentage of PUGs could be categorized as either unusually good or poor examples.

The Villeroy and Boch craftsmen were well trained in superior transfer printing techniques soon after the factory in Mettlach was opened. The English are generally credited with developing the processes used, and V&B artisans provided excellent examples of this technique, especially on some early plates. In 1880

Fig. 14 715(1909) .5L, 1008(1909) .5L, 1107(2271) .5L

American craftsmen at the famous Rookwood factory in Cincinnati, Ohio produced a rich dark brown backgrounded glazed ware that the V&B craftsmen also began to imitate. These Mettlach wares were decorated using hand painting

as well as the atomizer spraying of colored slips that was invented at Rookwood for decorative shadings. This extra attention would account for the fact that the Mettlach *Rookwood* wares originally sold for more than similar etched items. Many of the decorations on these steins (Fig. 15) consisted of portraits of men, and they all carried decoration numbers in the 6000's. These decorations were painted onto special blank forms numbered from 2782 to 2793, and are listed in the catalog portion of this book according to the stein form numbers.

In their constant quest to revive the beauty and quality of Renaissance and Baroque ceramics the V&B craftsmen set to the task of copying the 17th and 18th Century faience steins, a European tin-glazed product meant to simulate the Oriental porcelains that were so popular and prohibitively expensive. The decorations on the Mettlach *faience* steins (Fig. 16) were primarily accomplished, with a few possible exceptions, via hand painting. One of the most outstanding characteristics of these steins, especially the 1-liter versions, is the use of

Fig. 15 2784/6129 2.2L

fancy and beautiful pewter mountings, i.e., the lids and footrings. This pewter-work greatly enhances the authentic appearance of these faience steins. The designs are probably not exact copies of designs on ancient faience steins, but there are distinct similarities to original designs, so much so that in some cases particular faience factories can be associated with the styles of several of the Mettlach items. Mettlach produced a number of other types of faience wares but the steins seem to have been the most popular.

Another ware that also involved hand painting (except for stein 5013/965 which was a PUG) was the Mettlach revival of the *Delft*-type decorations. Although the technique was virtually identical to that used in the faience replicas, the use of blue and white designs and the use of decorative devices typical of the famous antique Delft wares, makes them easily distinguishable from the faience replicas. The Delft style (Fig. 17) was used on a very wide variety of Mettlach wares.

Fig. 16 5442 1.0L   Fig. 17 Plaque 5159

2.4 Etched or Chromolith

When the name *Mettlach* is recognized, it is mostly associated with the beautiful *chromolith* steins (Fig. 18). This was as much true 100 years ago as it is today, for it was the chromolith steins that brought to the Villeroy and Boch Mettlach factory the awards and acclaims that boosted it into the category of an extraordinary manufacturer. Even though by most accounts these products are considered *mass produced,* they are recognized as being among the finest quality items of their type.

Chromolith, or *colored stone,* was the name preferred by V&B, but the simpler term *etched* has become so universally utilized that there is no changing it now. Actually the chromolith wares were not etched, rather the design was made by some form of a mold or pressed process. The 1921 fire at the Mettlach factory destroyed some of the equipment used for making the chromolith wares. That process, however was apparently so labor intensive and costly that it was not worthwhile to go back into full-scale production after the fire and the economic and wartime disruptions. Some people are of the opinion that the chromolith production was a breakeven or marginally unprofitable operation even in the best of times. At any rate the process was not revived, except for occasional production of special orders, such as etched stein 2900, which ceased in the early 1930's.

Fig. 18 3099 3.0L

With no tangible evidence other than *autopsies* of broken pieces, there have been a number of theories advanced to explain the process for making the chromolith products. As with the production techniques for all the other types of Mettlach wares, there is no categorical proof of which production techniques were used. The information advanced in this book is thus more or less speculative; it would be a disservice to readers not to provide information about current conjectures.

There are some elements that are common to many of the chromolith theories. The design is generally recognized to be a separate section which was applied and fused to the body with pressure and great heat. The hard white glaze on the interior was applied separately and vitrified during one of the firings. While it would appear that the design materials were wrapped around the body, there are some knowledgeable researchers who feel that the body could have been poured into the design.

The V&B literature that was used to promote the sale of chromolith products would tend to suggest that colored clays were laid into the body of the wares in a process similar to cloisonne. In fact, previous to 1880 it is known from Mettlach records that have survived that some chromolith wares were made for royal and noble houses that were extraordinarily beautiful but accomplished in such a labor-intensive process that it would have been impossible to produce or sell any quantities. This could well have been that *inlaid* process, sometimes called *true chromolith.* The acclaim for these items was however, so extraordinary that the V&B craftsmen set to the task of inventing a more reasonable way of achieving similar results. In 1880 it is known that they did develop such a process and began the widespread marketing of their highly acclaimed etched wares.

The *inlaid* theory is advanced by some, even for the mass-produced items. However, those who have examined broken pieces of etched wares know that the color is only a 64th of an inch or less in depth. As a consequence of this shallow depth some people subscribe to a theory of *staining* or *painting* with a colored agent or slip clay. The staining theory seems to break down due to the absolute uniformity of colors in large areas, and the painting theory runs into trouble due to the perfectly smooth, brushstroke free, surface of these items.

A *reverse painting* theory seems to be picking up more support lately, and it claims the following. A flat or curved tray was developed which had the etched lines in reverse, that is protruding, from its surface. Colored clay slips were hand painted onto this, perhaps plaster or metal, tray. Colors for which atomizer sprayed shadings were required, such as the background of stein 2134, were sprayed after all other colors had been painted, and then painted over with the solid background color. An eighth inch, or so, layer of slip or moist stoneware was then placed on the tray and the decoration was lifted from the design tray and set into the appropriate portion of a body or a body mold. The rest of the body had already, or was then, poured or hand worked into its mold, which was then cleaned on a potter's wheel.

In virtually all theories it is believed that the handle was applied separately on most of the steins. Bases were sometimes also applied, but the frieze bands are generally felt to be integral to the body of steins. After the decoration had been fired it is usually believed that the black lines, that form the distinctive outlining in the decoration, were produced by rubbing a black glaze into the incised lines. Since these black lines are often missing in back near the handle it is sometimes felt that the handle, and perhaps the frieze bands, were in their highly absorbent bisque stage during the blacking. They may have been decorated with their shiny or matte glazes at the same stage as the *blacking* and fired at the same time. While the decoration is generally finished in a *matte* glaze, possibly before the blacking, there are some steins which have a heavy, *shiny* glaze, such as steins which have large areas that were painted from the outside with colored glazes, e.g. 1786 and 2717. In addition to these occasional shiny glazes, colored matte glazes were sometimes hand painted onto steins to provide shadings and highlights that would be difficult to reverse paint, or to provide colors that could only survive the lower firing temperatures used for glazes, such as the reds.

The earliest etched wares, those produced in the 1880's, tend to have more etching, more precise etching, more colors (in some cases as many as twenty), and less heavy glazing of handles, lips, bases, and other parts external to the design. By 1905 the prolific use of colors, shadings, and intricate designs had subsided substantially, perhaps as a means of controlling the costs of making these items.

Even on different examples of the same piece there can be substantial differences in the quality of the etching, in the care with which hand painting and glazing were conducted, and in the significance of the almost universally present *factory flaws*. Minor flakes often occurred on the bands and handles; if they took place at the bisque stage the colored glazes partially masked them. Minor separations of the clay, often called firing lines, were commonplace, and although they were quite shallow they usually picked up a darker color or the blacking glaze. A more thorough discussion of factory-introduced, and consumer-introduced, flaws and their effects on the value and desirability of various pieces is presented in Appendix A.

Of greatest importance in determining the desirability of etched steins is the nature of the design. In fact there are four types of designs that are significantly less desirable than other etched steins, and are commonly known only by the following designations. The *art nouveau* wares (Fig. 19) are etched with the bold sinuous designs that became so popular at the beginning of the 20th Century. The designs are often dominated by either a blue and tan or a rust and green color scheme. The *mosaic* wares (Fig. 20) generally followed the relief era and preceded the etched era. Although some mosaic pieces contain etched sections, for the most part they were totally decorated with colored glazes on surfaces that are actually quite complex compared to the usual etched pieces. The *glazed* wares are similar to mosaics but have no protrusions from the surface. The relative undesirability of most of the mosaic and glazed pieces is due more to the simple, repetitive, floral and geometric designs than to a disenchantment with the results of the techinques themselves. In fact some of the most desirable steins are glazed-type steins with very wonderful figures and scenes (2717 or 2720, for example). The final important sub-category under *etched* are the *tapestry* steins (Fig. 21). These steins generally have an etched portrait-like section on the front of the stein with a large grey undecorated, or sparsely decorated, area on the sides and back.

Fig. 19 2912 2.0L

Fig. 20 1789 .5L

Fig. 21 1645 .5L

It would be redundant to describe all the different combinations of techniques that were ever tried at Mettlach. Cameo and etched, relief and etched, and almost every other combination can be found. One variant that does deserve some note is the *full color relief,* which appears to be the relief technique filled in from the back with colored slips. Here again it is the subject matter that primarily determines the desirability of wares that contain full color relief portions, from the relatively undesirable full color relief tapestries, such as 1756 to 1759, to the very desirable full color relief and etched steins, such as 2917 (Fig. 22) and 3329.

Variations in the coloring or decoration of Mettlach wares are generally not very important. Stein 2693 can, for example, be found with two variations of scroll designs. Steins 2716 and 2640 (Fig. 23) can be found with either German or English wording. Steins 1527 and 2100 can be found with major differences in the colors that were used. These are all relatively unimportant variations. An important variation would be a *Probe* sample design (Fig. 24) for a highly desirable item that had a substantially different design then the ultimate *production* model (there is such an example of stein 2238).

Fig. 22 2917 .5L

Fig. 23 2640 .5L German
and English versions

2.5 Lids on Steins

Etched, mosaic, relief, and cameo steins are found most frequently with inlaid lids, and these are almost without exception (the 1786 is an exception) the most desirable lids to the collectors. Actually the so-called *inlaid* lid is a decorated stoneware disk that has been set into a pewter rim. For almost all steins that came with inlaid lids, the design on the ceramic insert is an extension

Fig. 24
2238 .5L
production
model and
Probe
design

of the colors and designs used in the body of the stein, and thus there is only one
inlaid lid that is appropriate for that stein. A rare exception is the *Trumpeter
from Sackingen* series, 2007, 2008, and 2009, in which the three different lids
were often interchanged (Fig. 25). In many of the series, the steins all share a
common inlaid lid design; on most of the rest of the series the lids are similar but
pick up design elements particular to the various steins (such as in the 3089 to
3093 series). A very few steins that had simple inlays are often found with other
simple inlays, perhaps it was a matter of expediency during production.

As fanatic as some collectors are about inlaid lids one would think that these
were the only genuine lids. Actually a variety of genuine lids existed. Many
steins could be ordered without lids (although this must have been rare except
for those who wanted to add their own), with inlaid ceramic lids, with flat or
somewhat domed plain pewter lids, or with fancy pewter lids such as the steeple

Fig. 25 Three Different lids from 2007, 2008 and 2009 series

shaped or flatter relief scenes. It is true that not all of these options were available for all steins, but they were for the majority of the etched steins.

Plain pewter lids originally cost about as much as the ceramic inlays, but with fancy pewter lids the steins were 5 to 15% more expensive. Appendix A offers some further comments on the current desirability and value of steins with various types of lids. The prices in the following section of this book are predicated on the steins having the type of lid noted. Steins with fancy pewter lids can often be gotten for significant discounts, and aesthetically, particularly in displays, people often claim to prefer them. This apparent contradiction has been fostered by some myths about authenticity, concerns about the difficulties of recognizing replaced pewter lids, the rarity of fancy pewter lids and the difficulties involved in putting together a collection of them, and other self-perpetuating reasons such as feelings about their acceptability among the collectors who form the market for steins.

2.6 Thumblifts and Hinges

Although the majority of steins seem to have been produced with just one specific thumblift (Fig. 26), some authentic variations do exist. The 2091 could have a fireman or a flame; 2133 and 2134 could have a gnome or a jester. A United States shield thumblift is often seen on steins made for export to this country, even when the subject matter of the stein is unrelated to the United States. Generally the only way to determine whether or not a thumblift is original is to examine its base for evidence of a repair, such as soldering or filing.

Most hinges on Mettlach steins have five rings. Steins made prior to about 1890 may have only three rings, while the very large steins often have seven-ringed hinges. Inconsistencies from these generalities have no bearing on the desirability of a particular stein. Some of the pewterwork was done in the town of Mettlach by the Wagner factory. Other pewterwork may have regularly been added elsewhere outside the Mettlach factory or, possibly, in a distinctly independent operation within the factory. Some of the really fancy original pewter lids have been found with the incised marks of Munich pewterers such as Pauson or Lichtinger. Refer to Appendix A.7 for information about pewter lids.

Fig. 26 Examples of thumblifts on Mettlach steins

2.7 Artists, Designs, and Sets

Some Mettlach steins and plaques carry the name or initials of the artist (Fig. 27) who was responsible for the original artwork from which the design was copied. Many of the Mettlach items do not carry this so-called *signature* of an artist and cannot be attributed to a known artist by their style. The most prolific artists were Christian Warth, who became director of the art department, Heinrich Schlitt, Fritz Quidenus, M. Hein, and Johann Baptist Stahl. Stahl's designs appear only on phanolith, cameo, and relief wares. Hein designed mosaic and etched wares as well as some full color relief steins. The names Warth and Quidenus are generally found only on etched pieces, and Schlitt's work can be found on etched and PUG wares. While some of the designs probably originated from other work intended for a purpose of its own, such as murals by Schlitt that have shown up as stein designs, most of the decorations were created by Mettlach artists or commissioned artists specifically for use on Mettlach wares.

Some collectors seek out *signed* pieces, but they do so because the artist, usually Schlitt, has created decorations that particularly appeal to that individual collector. It should be noted that the signature or initials were part of the design of every example of that stein or plaque (with the exception of stein 2455 for which a signed and unsigned mold both existed). Whether or not an item is signed will have little bearing on the desirability of that item, many signed pieces are relatively inexpensive, while a large percentage of the most desirable items are not signed.

Pairs and large sets of items can be found in various styles of Mettlach wares including etched, cameo, phanolith, relief, PUG, glazed, and other types. The sets can also come from different types of wares; there are steins that match steins, plaques that match steins, mustard pots that match salad bowls, and almost any other imaginable combination. The catalog sections of this book note many of these relationships because they are very important to collectors.

Although they are somewhat rarer there are examples of matching items that involve different production techniques. For example, etched plaques 2621 to 2626 match etched coasters 2817 to 2822 as well as the PUG beakers with decorations 1091 to 1096 (Fig. 28). Another example involves etched stein 2767 which matches the PUG plaque with decoration 1014 and the PUG stein with decoration 1014.

As a general rule the pairs and sets are consecutively numbered, or they had a single number plus letters A, B, and so on. Where the sets are not consecutively numbered it is clear that either (1) it was difficult to line up the completion of different types of pieces, such as master steins that are within about 100 numbers of the individual steins, or (2) the making of the set was clearly an afterthought, such as with steins 2024 and 3043.

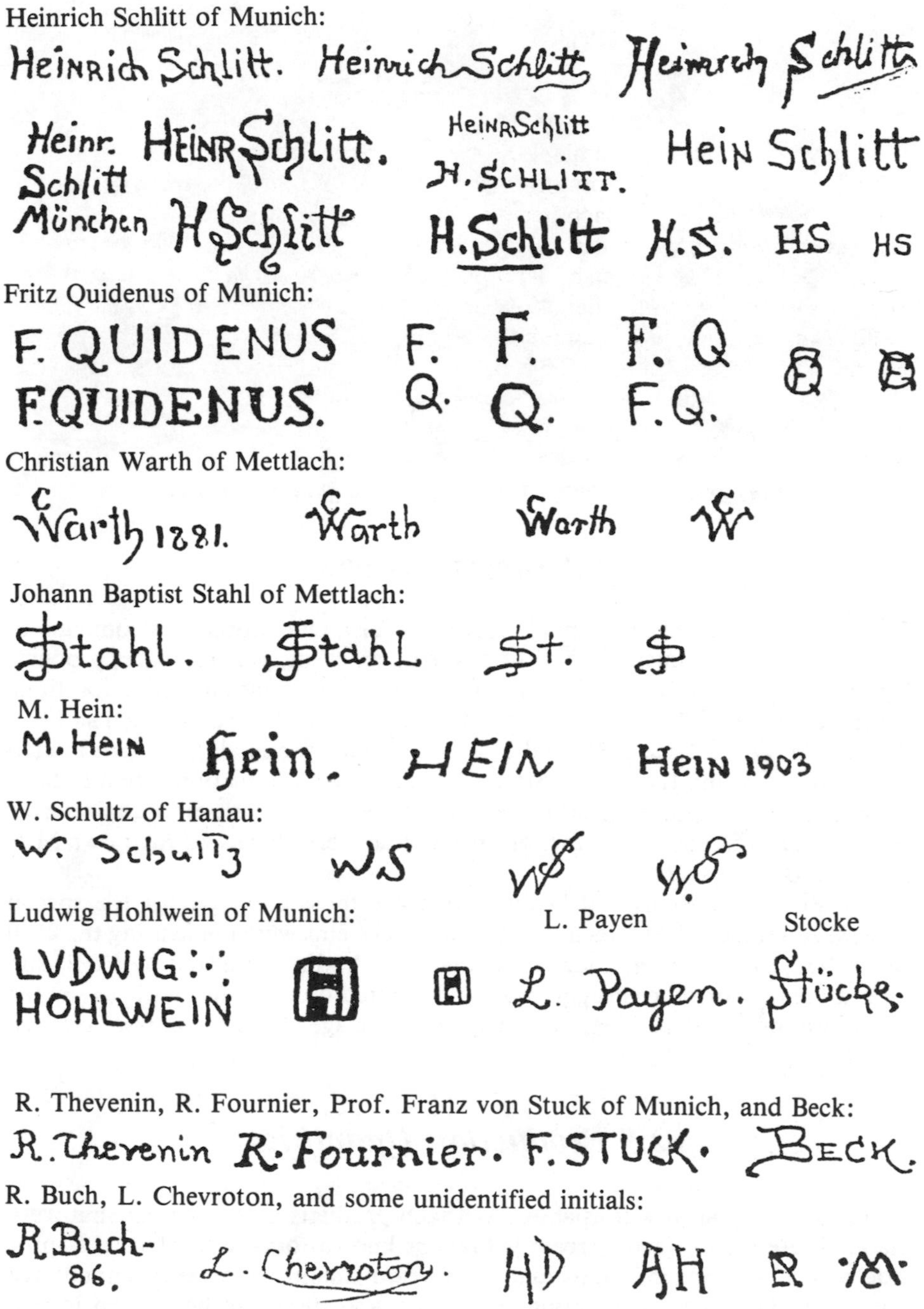

Heinrich Schlitt of Munich:

Heinrich Schlitt.   Heinrich Schlitt,   Heinrich Schlitt

Heinr. HEINRSchlitt.   HeinRSchlitt   Hein Schlitt
Schlitt   H. SCHLITT.
München HSchlitt'   H.Schlitt   H.S.   HS   HS

Fritz Quidenus of Munich:

F. QUIDENUS   F.   F.   F. Q
F.QUIDENUS.   Q.   Q.   F.Q.

Christian Warth of Mettlach:

Warth 1881.   Warth   Warth   W

Johann Baptist Stahl of Mettlach:

Stahl.   Stahl   St.   S

M. Hein:

M.Hein   Hein.   HEIN   Hein 1903

W. Schultz of Hanau:

W. Schultz   WS   WS   WS

Ludwig Hohlwein of Munich: L. Payen   Stocke

LVDWIG:.:   ⊞   ⊞   L. Payen.   Stücke.
HOHLWEIN

R. Thevenin, R. Fournier, Prof. Franz von Stuck of Munich, and Beck:

R. Thevenin   R. Fournier.   F.STUCK.   BECK.

R. Buch, L. Chevroton, and some unidentified initials:

R.Buch-   L. Chevroton.   HD   AH   R   M
86.

Fig. 27 Examples of some artists' "signatures" on Mettlach wares

Fig. 28 Coaster 2822, Plaque 2626, Beaker 1094(2368)

2.8 Special Orders

Many Mettlach items were made especially for an individual or a company to help commemorate, memorialize, or advertise an event, person, place, product, business, or organization. It seems that the most common outlet for these special orders was the American market. Even some etched steins, such as 1997, 2238, 2373, 2871, 2872, 3135, and 3156, were made for small groups or limited retail outlets within the United States. Special order productions seem to have been quite easily handled since there were scores of universities, organizations, breweries, restaurants, and other businesses that were able to get their own Mettlach steins or beakers.

The PUG-style steins and beakers were the most common for the special orders. A number of Mettlach regimental PUG steins were made using the 2140 blank body. In addition, countless blank PUG bodies were sold by V&B, and later a brewery or other insignia was cold painted onto them, that is to say the design was not fired in. There is no way to tell the age of the decorations on such pieces.

2.9 Production Quantities

One of the great mysteries about Mettlach products is the number that were made. There are no factory records that are known to have survived that provide any accounting of individual production quantities or even cumulative quantities. There can thus only be estimates, and these can be derived in two ways. First, the cost of the wares, the wage rates, and the number of workers can be used to guess at the number of hours of labor required per item and then possibly the number of items. The second method of estimation is through observation and speculation as to the fraction of the extant pieces that are likely to cross the market over some time period.

As for the second method of estimation, over the years I have kept records of the steins and other wares that I have sold, others have sold, or that I have appraised, seen, or heard about. Initially I felt that the rarity of certain pieces would be a measure of the level and volatility of their prices. This has not been the case, since, obviously, the unattractive steins were infrequently ordered, and even today they are undesirable, so they are relatively inexpensive. I continued to keep careful records because I became curious about the production quantities.

Steins with fewer than 10 that have surfaced in the last decade I consider to be *extremely rare*. There are actually very few *desirable* steins that fall into this category, it is predominately populated by steins such as the tree-trunk types, early glazed, advertising PUGs, and other less attractive varieties. For steins of which 10 to 30 examples have become known, the *rare* steins, there are perhaps a few dozen desirable examples. *Moderately rare* steins, I feel, are those of which 30 to 50 have surfaced in this past decade. The majority of the Mettlach steins and plaques are in the *common* area of 100 to 500 examples, with the *most common* having significantly more than 500. Although I don't keep careful records of anything other than the prices once there are more than 50 to 100 that I have seen, I can recall a couple dozen steins that are certainly in the *most common* category.

Naturally these numbers do not include all of the Mettlach items that exist in the United States, nor for the roughly comparable number that exist in Germany and the rest of the world. With additional years of observation, however, the steins in each of these various categories have changed little. If this continues to be the case, and in a couple of years there is a revision of this price guide, it would then seem appropriate to provide collectors with information about the relative rarity of each of the steins.

Estimations of the number of steins originally produced are fraught with even more uncertainties. A *tremendous* number of steins were destroyed over the years, particularly during the wars. There are any number of soldiers who have recalled machine-gunning hundreds of shelves full of steins throughout Germany — apparently this had become an important cathartic form of cultural vandalism for the invading forces. This destruction has made the U.S. inventory an important fraction of the current world supply. Based partly upon the extrapolation back from recent observations, and partly from the use of cost and wage figures, it seems improbable that the average production of Mettlach wares could have exceeded 2000 examples. The *most common* items, however, definitely had more than 2000 produced, perhaps 10,000 or more. In the case of the *extremely rare* steins (Fig. 29) and plaques it seems unlikely that more than 100 were ever produced.

Fig. 29 285 1.0L, most of
the hand painted steins
are extremely rare.

3119 1.0L, an extremely
rare stein, value with
pewter lid as shown $1800.

3. Steins by Incised Mold Number

The steins that Villeroy & Boch/Mettlach produced certainly have been the most famous and popular of their wares. All the many different styles of steins that have *incised* mold, or form, numbers are listed here in numerical order. The print under glaze, PUG, steins that carry the *printed* decoration numbers are listed in the next section, even if they happen to also carry an incised mold number. The inconsistent marking system and occasionally identical incised and printed numbers, have caused a cataloging problem which seems most expediently solved by the use of these separate stein sections. A tremendous amount of duplicate listing is thus avoided, and with the reader's indulgence, some cross-referencing, the aid of photographs, and a little practice it is hoped that it will become easy to locate specific steins.

The so-called *Rookwood* series of Mettlach steins, with mold numbers from 2782 to 2793, are listed in this section under these numbers. The Mettlach Rookwood steins are so named because they closely resemble the Rookwood American Art pottery made in Cincinnati, Ohio around 1900. These steins have a rich brown background and are highly glazed; they are not considered to be PUG steins because their decoration appears to be hand painted.

Similarly the Mettlach faience-type steins were also mostly decorated by hand painting, and are also listed in this section according to their 5000-series numbers. As with the PUGs there is again an inconsistency in the marking of these steins. For numbers 5001 to 5034 the mold and decoration numbers are frequently the same. Later numbered faience steins carried unique and sequentially increasing decoration numbers, but occasionally are marked with earlier incised form numbers. Since these later decoration numbers are most descriptive and most frequently used, they are listed here as if they were form numbers. These Mettlach faience steins were made to resemble the 17th and 18th Century German faience steins, and better examples are much sought after.

Some of the very earliest steins made by Mettlach were unmarked or had trademarks that have worn or broken off. Frequently they were unnumbered or the number was incorporated into the center of the trademark. Many of these steins resemble a tree trunk, produced with ceramic material that is dark brown mottled with tan and green lines. On occasion they have a shiny, somewhat worn, platinum accenting. While not common, these steins have not achieved a very high demand nor a high price, perhaps because of lack of knowledge or lack of aesthetic appeal. Usually found in ½-liter sizes these steins range in price between $125 and $200, slightly higher for larger sizes. Most of these pieces will not be listed here.

The names of the artists occasionally are included in the design around the body of the stein and other Mettlach wares. On the steins these names are listed in full, in part, or as initials, but for convenience many of these are indicated in the descriptions of the pieces as *signed* with the artist's last name.

Number	Size	Type	Lid	Description	Value
6	1.5L	Relief	Inlay	Three panels, front scene is woman with shield and sword	$200.
6	2.5L	Relief	Inlay	(master to 1266)	$225.
6	3.1L	Relief	Inlay		$225.
7	1.1L	Relief	Pewter	Barley design	$125.
7	1.5L	Relief	Pewter		$160.
7	2.1L	Relief	Pewter		$200.

32 .5L   171 .25L   328 .5L

228 .5L, 282 .5L, 485 1.0L

Number	Size	Type	Lid	Description	Value
8	2.1L	Relief	Pewter	Roses	$225.
24	.5L	Relief	Inlay	Figures in four separate panels	$250.
24	1.0L	Relief	Inlay		$325.
32	.5L	Relief	Inlay	Body simulates castle, three panels, Gambrinus	$300.
62	.5L	Hand Painted	Pewter	Fraternal crest	$200.
171	.25L	Relief	Inlay	Figures representing activity during twelve months	$150.
171	.5L	Relief	Inlay		$175.
171	3.2L	Relief	Inlay		$325.
202	.5L	Relief	Inlay	Group of men singing	$250.
202	1.0L	Relief	Inlay		$300.
202	1.0L	Relief	Inlay	With gnome on inlay	$500.
216	.5L	Relief	Inlay	Tree trunk style, leaves and vines with platinum coloring	$175.
228	.5L	Relief	Inlay	Four panels, musical scenes	$250.
280	.5L	Hand Painted	Pewter	Fraternal crest	$200.
280	.5L	PUG	Pewter	Print under glaze blank body (see PUG Steins)	—

Number	Size	Type	Lid	Description	Value
282	.5L	Hand Painted	Pewter	Fraternal crest	$200.
285	1.0L	Hand Painted	Pewter	Prussian eagle	$500.
285	1.0L	Hand Painted	Pewter	Blank body number used for hand painting	—
328	.5L	Relief	Inlay	Drunken steins, hat on inlay	$275.
368	.5L	Relief	Inlay	Leaves and vines, simulates tree	$175.
385	.5L	Relief	Pewter	Fraternal crest, full color relief	$250.
386	.5L	Hand Painted	Pewter	Fraternal crest	$250.

62 .5L, 280 .5L, 385 .5L

Number	Size	Type	Lid	Description	Value
403	.5L	Relief	Pewter	Fraternal crest, full color relief	$250.
406	.5L	Hand Painted	Pewter	Fraternal crest	$175.
406	.5L	Hand Painted	Pewter	Crest of the State of California	$500.
406	.5L	Hand Painted	Pewter	Regimental: *Luftschiffer* 1893-1895, balloon on front	$1800.
406	.5L	Hand Painted	Pewter	Portrait of A. Durer	$350.
406	.5L	Hand Painted	Pewter	Blank body number used for hand painting	—

386 .5L   403 .5L   406 *Luftschiffer* .5L

Number	Size	Type	Lid	Description	Value
409	2.7L	Relief	Inlay	Four panels, drinking scenes	$375.
485	.5L	Relief	Inlay	Musicians, dancers	$250.
485	1.0L	Relief	Inlay		$325.
485	.5L	Relief	Inlay	With gnome on inlay	$500.
675	.25L	Relief	Inlay	Barrel shape	$85.
675	.5L	Relief	Inlay		$125.

675 .5L, 783 .5L, 812 .5L

Number	Size	Type	Lid	Description	Value
690	1.6L	Relief	Inlay	Barrel shape	$175.
690	2.5L	Relief	Inlay		$200.
690	4.0L	Relief	Inlay		$225.
699	2.25L	Relief	Pewter	Woman playing musical instrument	$275.
762	1.5L	Relief	Inlay	Leaves	$200.
783	.5L	Relief	Inlay	Children on beer barrel, *Bock Bier*	$250.
809	.5L	Relief	Inlay	*Bacchus*	$225.
809	1.0L	Relief	Inlay		$300.
812	.5L	Relief	Inlay	Hunters	$250.
812	1.0L	Relief	Inlay		$325.
812	1.85L	Relief	Pewter	With horn shaped handle	$450.
814	1.0L	Relief	Inlay	Four panels	$275.
815	1.3L	Relief	Pewter	Floral design	$250.
817	.5L	Relief	Inlay	Floral design and rams	$175.
818	.9L	Relief	Inlay	Children playing	$250.
818	1.1L	Relief	Inlay		$325.
819	.45L	Relief	Pewter	Wheat design	$135.
819	.6L	Relief	Pewter		$150.
819	1.0L	Relief	Pewter		$175.
819	2.1L	Relief	Pewter		$200.
819	3.0L	Relief	Pewter		$250.
1000	.32L	Relief	Inlay	Medallions	$125.
1002	2.5L	Relief	Pewter	Men drinking	$300.
1005	.5L	Relief	Inlay	Tavern scenes	$250.
1005	1.0L	Relief	Inlay		$325.
1006	4.5L	Relief	Inlay	Small designs with people all around body of stein, gargoyle pouring lip with hanging ring	$475.
1027	1.0L	Relief	Inlay	Floral design	$175.
1028	.5L	Relief	Inlay	Background like tree trunk, man carrying hay, walking with woman	$150.
1028	2.3L	Relief	Inlay		$275.
1028	4.0L	Relief	Inlay		$325.
1035	1.5L	Mosaic	Inlay	Geometric design (master to 1036)	$250.
1035	2.5L	Mosaic	Inlay		$300.
1036	.3L	Mosaic	Inlay	Geometric design (master is 1035)	$150.
1036	.5L	Mosaic	Inlay		$200.

Number	Size	Type	Lid	Description	Value
1037	.3L	Relief	Inlay	Man drinking	$120.
1037	.5L	Relief	Inlay		$150.
1052	1.0L	Etched	Inlay	Shield and winged horses	$500.
1053	1.0L	Etched	Inlay	Dwarfs drinking, full color	$800.
1053	1.0L	Etched	Inlay	Dwarfs drinking, mono-color	$650.
1054	.3L	Mosaic	Inlay	Floral design	$160.
1055	.6L	Mosaic	Inlay	Floral design (master is 1057)	$250.
1055	1.3L	Mosaic	Inlay		$325.
1057	4.0L	Etched & Mosaic	Inlay	Cherubs, flowers (master to 1055)	$475.
1059	.5L	Relief	Inlay	Geometric design	$200.

817 .5L, 1005 1.0L   1028 .5L

Number	Size	Type	Lid	Description	Value
1060	.3L	Relief	Inlay	Barrel-like (master is 1112)	$130.
1060	.5L	Relief	Inlay		$175.
1062	.5L	Mosaic	Inlay	Geometric design (master is 1063)	$250.
1063	2.6L	Mosaic	Inlay	Geometric design (master to 1062)	$450.
1065	3.5L	Etched & Mosaic	Inlay	Cherubs and geometric design (master to 1068)	$600.
1066	2.3L	Relief	Inlay	Geometric design (master to 1084)	$425.

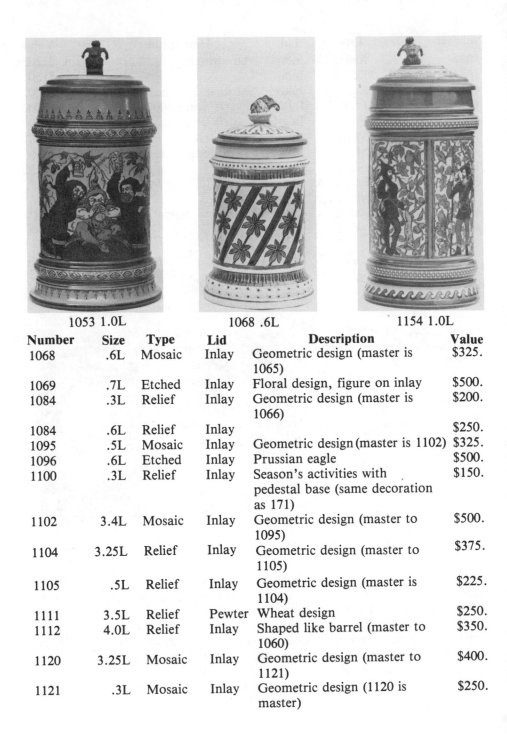

| 1053 1.0L | 1068 .6L | 1154 1.0L |

Number	Size	Type	Lid	Description	Value
1068	.6L	Mosaic	Inlay	Geometric design (master is 1065)	$325.
1069	.7L	Etched	Inlay	Floral design, figure on inlay	$500.
1084	.3L	Relief	Inlay	Geometric design (master is 1066)	$200.
1084	.6L	Relief	Inlay		$250.
1095	.5L	Mosaic	Inlay	Geometric design (master is 1102)	$325.
1096	.6L	Etched	Inlay	Prussian eagle	$500.
1100	.3L	Relief	Inlay	Season's activities with pedestal base (same decoration as 171)	$150.
1102	3.4L	Mosaic	Inlay	Geometric design (master to 1095)	$500.
1104	3.25L	Relief	Inlay	Geometric design (master to 1105)	$375.
1105	.5L	Relief	Inlay	Geometric design (master is 1104)	$225.
1111	3.5L	Relief	Pewter	Wheat design	$250.
1112	4.0L	Relief	Inlay	Shaped like barrel (master to 1060)	$350.
1120	3.25L	Mosaic	Inlay	Geometric design (master to 1121)	$400.
1121	.3L	Mosaic	Inlay	Geometric design (1120 is master)	$250.

Number	Size	Type	Lid	Description	Value
1123	2.0L	Relief	None	Pearlized glaze, figure holding up pouring spout, ewer shaped	$650.
1124	2.0L	Etched	None	Portrait of man on one side and woman on reverse, signed Warth	$1000.
1130	.5L	Etched	Inlay	*Munich guard beaker*	$550.
1131	.5L	Etched	Inlay	Tavern scene (mate to 1149)	$550.
1132	.5L	Etched	Inlay	Man fiddling and dancing crocodile in front of pyramids	$650.
1133	.5L	Mosaic	Inlay	Geometric design	$350.
1144	.5L	Relief	Inlay	Race horses	$275.
1146	.5L	Etched	Inlay	Students drinking in tavern, signed Warth	$475.
1147	4.6L	Relief & Mosaic	Inlay	Geometric design with medallions in relief	$475.
1148	.5L	Mosaic	Inlay	Geometric design	$350.
1149	.5L	Etched	Inlay	Man using large scale (mate to 1131)	$475.
1151	.5L	Relief	Inlay	Bulbous, with medallions around center (master is 1152)	$200.
1152	5.5L	Etched & Relief	Pewter	Small etched Prussian eagle, relief figures, and medallions around stein (master to 1151)	$525.
1153	4.0L	Relief	Inlay	Geometric design	$475.
1154	1.0L	Etched	Inlay	Hunting scenes, four panels	$800.
1154	1.0L	Relief	Pewter	Yale University emblem	$275.
1155	.5L	Mosaic	Inlay	Geometric design	$250.

1096 .6L, 1130 .5L, 1155 .5L

Number	Size	Type	Lid	Description	Value
1157	1.0L	Relief	Inlay	Cavaliers in four panels	$350.
1159	6.2L	Etched	Pewter	Four dancing and musical scenes	$1600.
1161	7.0L	Etched	Inlay	Two ladies, shields of German states, Prussian eagle, crown on lid, signed Warth (master to 1986)	$4300.
1161	7.0L	Etched	Pewter	Same, with pewter lid	$2800.

1123 2.0L, 1124 2.0L

Number	Size	Type	Lid	Description	Value
1162	.5L	Etched	Inlay	Three panels, dancing, signed Warth	$475.
1163	.5L	Etched	Inlay	Musicians, signed Warth (same as 1471 except different background)	$475.
1164	.5L	Etched	Inlay	Musician and girl	$475.
1169	2.5L	Relief	Inlay	Medallions, Nurnberg artists (master to 1184, matches pokal 1247)	$500.
1174	3.5L	Relief	Inlay	Geometric design (master to 1261)	$425.

1131 .5L pewter lid: value $550., 1132 .5L, 1149 .5L

Number	Size	Type	Lid	Description	Value
1175	2.0L	Mosaic	None	Geometric design	$275.
1180	.5L	Relief	Inlay	Drinking verse	$140.
1184	.3L	Relief	Inlay	Floral design (master is 1169)	$165.
1188	.6L	Mosaic	Inlay	Geometric design	$350.
1189	.6L	Mosaic	Inlay	Geometric design	$350.
1190	.5L	Mosaic	Inlay	Geometric design	$375.
1191	.6L	Mosaic	Inlay	Geometric design	$375.
1192	.6L	Mosaic	Inlay	Geometric design	$375.

1146 .5L   1162 .5L   1164 .5L

1258 .5L

1288 .5L

1286 3.1L

1161 7.0L

1313 3.1L

Number	Size	Type	Lid	Description	Value
1217	3.0L	Etched	None	Nine Faust opera scenes	$850.
1219	1.5L	Mosaic	Pewter	Geometric design	$300.
1221	1.5L	Mosaic	Inlay	Geometric design	$300.
1222	.5L	Mosaic	Inlay	Floral design	$350.
1223	.5L	Relief	Inlay	Geometric design (master is 1236)	$325.
1224	.6L	Mosaic	Inlay	Floral design	$375.
1225	2.0L	Relief	None	Geometric design	$375.
1227	.5L	Mosaic	Inlay	Geometric design	$350.
1228	.5L	Etched	Inlay	Sailboats	$575.
1236	3.1L	Relief	Inlay	Geometric design (master to 1223)	$425.
1246	4.0L	Relief	None	Grecian scene, gargoyle spout	$700.
1257	3.1L	Mosaic	Inlay	Floral design (master to 1258)	$450.
1258	.5L	Mosaic	Inlay	Floral design (master is 1257)	$350.
1261	.5L	Mosaic	Inlay	Geometric design (master is 1174)	$275.

1224 .6L, 1300 .6L, 1353 .6L

Number	Size	Type	Lid	Description	Value
1265	.25L	Relief	Inlay	Crests	$150.
1266	.25L	Relief	Inlay	Three panels, drinking scenes (master is 6)	$120.
1266	.5L	Relief	Inlay		$160.
1284	3.0L	Mosaic	Inlay	Geometric design (master to 1293)	$500.
1286	3.1L	Mosaic	Inlay	Floral design (master to 1288)	$475.
1287	4.0L	Relief	None	Faces in medallions	$600.

Number	Size	Type	Lid	Description	Value
1288	.5L	Mosaic	Inlay	Floral design (master is 1286)	$300.
1293	.5L	Mosaic	Inlay	Geometric design (master is 1284)	$350.
1298	.3L	Mosaic	Inlay	Geometric design (master is 1406)	$325.
1300	.6L	Relief	Inlay	Medallions around stein	$300.
1313	3.1L	Mosaic	Inlay	Geometric design (master to 1314)	$475.
1314	.5L	Mosaic	Inlay	Geometric design (master is 1313)	$350.
1333	1.1L	Mosaic	Pewter	Floral design	$350.
1338	1.1L	Mosaic	Inlay	Floral design	$375.
1352	3.1L	Mosaic	Inlay	Floral design (master to 1353)	$500.
1353	.6L	Mosaic	Inlay	Floral design (master is 1352)	$375.
1357	.25L	Mosaic	None	Floral design	$150.
1359	3.3L	Relief	Inlay	Floral design (master to 1363)	$450.
1363	.5L	Relief	Inlay	Floral design (master is 1359)	$225.
1366	2.0L	Relief	None	Floral design, bird under handle	$475.
1367	4.6L	Mosaic	Inlay	Geometric design (master to 1419)	$475.
1370	.5L	Relief	Inlay	Floral design, verse	$170.
1379	.5L	Etched	Inlay	Four panels, architect related scenes	$700.

1379 .5L, 1394 .5L, 1395 .5L

| 1403 .5L | 1454 .5L | 1467 .5L |

Number	Size	Type	Lid	Description	Value
1394	.5L	Etched	Inlay	German card stein (mate to 1395)	$500.
1395	.5L	Etched	Inlay	French card stein (mate to 1394)	$500.
1396	.5L	Etched	Inlay	Nymph drinking out of large stein, signed Warth	$475.
1397	.6L	Etched	Inlay	Man with hat	$475.
1400	.4L	PUG	Inlay or Pewter	Print under glaze blank body (see PUG Steins)	—
1400	.5L	PUG	Inlay or Pewter		—
1402	.6L	Relief	Inlay	Geometric design	$225.
1403	.5L	Etched	Inlay	Man bowling in tavern, signed Warth	$500.
1406	3.1L	Mosaic	Inlay	Geometric design (master to 1298)	$450.
1419	.5L	Mosaic	Inlay	Geometric design (master is 1367)	$350.
1431	.4L	PUG	Inlay or Pewter	Print under glaze blank body (see PUG Steins)	—
1431	.5L	PUG	Inlay or Pewter		—
1431	1.0L	PUG	Inlay or Pewter		—

Number	Size	Type	Lid	Description	Value
1452	.3L	Mosaic	Inlay	Floral design (master is 1492)	$225.
1452	.5L	Mosaic	Inlay		$300.
1453	.5L	Etched	Inlay	Hunter, boars, and dogs (mate to 1823)	$600.
1454	.5L	Etched	Inlay	White horse in medallion	$500.
1455	1.4L	Mosaic	Pewter	Geometric design	$300.
1455	2.4L	Mosaic	Pewter		$375.
1459	.6L	Relief	Inlay	Verse	$160.
1460	.5L	Relief	Inlay	Horse in medallion, relief in full colors	$425.
1466	3.5L	Relief	Inlay	Cherubs (master to 1501)	$500.
1467	.5L	Relief	Inlay	Four panels: picking fruit, hunting, farming, weaving	$225.
1469	6.0L	Etched	Inlay	Gnomes celebrating (master to 1475 through 1480)	$1800.

1469 6.0L, 1690 4.5L

1476 .5L   1477 .5L   1479 .5L

Number	Size	Type	Lid	Description	Value
1471	.5L	Etched	Inlay	Musicians, signed Warth (same as 1163, except different background)	$475.
1472	.5L	Etched	Inlay	Cattle	$600.
			Set of Six		
1475	.5L	Etched	Inlay	Gnomes at work, in various stages of planting grapes and making wine (master is 1469)	$500.
1476	.5L	Etched	Inlay		$500.
1477	.5L	Etched	Inlay		$500.
1478	.5L	Etched	Inlay		$500.
1479	.5L	Etched	Inlay		$500.
1480	.5L	Etched	Inlay		$500.
1475-1480	.5L	Etched	Inlay	Same except gnome figurine on inlay	$1000.
1492	3.25L	Mosaic	Inlay	Floral design (master to 1452)	$425.
1493	1.5L	Relief	None	Floral design	$225.
1494	5.6L	Etched	Pewter	Man sitting on barrel and drinking beer, signed Warth (mate to 1498 and 1562, matches 2103)	$1600.
1498	5.6L	Etched	Pewter	Cavalier leaning on staff (mate to 1494 and 1562, matches 2104)	$1600.
1501	.5L	Relief	Inlay	Floral design (master is 1466)	$225.

1508 .5L   1519 .5L   1520 .5L

Number	Size	Type	Lid	Description	Value
~1508	.5L	Etched	Inlay	Tavern scene	$475.
1519	.5L	Etched	Inlay	Scull racing	$550.
1520	.5L	Etched	Inlay	Prussian eagle in front, soldiers on sides, signed Gorig	$575.
1521	.5L	Etched	Inlay	Three panels, child, cat, monkey	$500.
1525	.25L	Relief	Inlay	Shield on front	$170.

1521 .5L   1527 .5L   1532 .5L

Number	Size	Type	Lid	Description	Value
1526	.25L	PUG	Pewter	Print under glaze blank body (see PUG Steins)	—
1526	.3L	PUG	Pewter		—
1526	.4L	PUG	Pewter		—
1526	.5L	PUG	Pewter		—
1526	1.0L	PUG	Pewter		—
1526	3.0L	PUG	Pewter		—
1526	.5L	Relief	Pewter	Yale University	$150.
1527	.5L	Etched	Inlay	Four men drinking, sign'd Warth	$500.
1527	1.0L	Etched	Inlay		$650.

1494 5.6L, 1498 5.6L

Number	Size	Type	Lid	Description	Value
1530	.5L	PUG	Inlay	Print under glaze blank body (see PUG Steins)	—
1532	.5L	Etched	Inlay	Shield and rampant lions	$600.
1533	.5L	Tapestry	Pewter	Man drinking beer	$275.
1533	1.0L	Tapestry	Pewter		$325.
1536	.5L	Tapestry	Pewter	Man with pipe	$275.
1536	1.0L	Tapestry	Pewter		$325.
1539	.3L	Mosaic	Inlay	Floral design	$250.
1562	5.65L	Etched	Pewter	*Trumpeter of Sackingen* (mate to 1494 and 1498, matches 2105, master to 1998)	$1600.

1562 5.65L

1570 .5L

1577 4.5L, 1578 4.5L

Number	Size	Type	Lid	Description	Value
1566	.5L	Etched	Inlay	Man on high wheel bicycle, signed Gorig	$900.
1568	6.0L	Relief	None	Busts of Wagner	$1200.
1569	2.5L	Mosaic	Inlay	Geometric design, ewer shape	$525.
1570	.5L	Mosaic	Inlay	Leaf design, signed Hein	$350.
1571	2.0L	Mosaic	Inlay	Floral design	$425.
1577	4.5L	Etched	Pewter	Twelve people in dinner scene (mate to 1578)	$2000.
1578	4.5L	Etched	Pewter	Tavern scene (mate to 1577)	$2000.
1625	1.0L	Mosaic	Inlay	Geometric design	$300.
1632	5.0L	Etched	Inlay	Drinking scenes on both sides, ewer shape, signed Warth and Hein	$2100.
1637	1.5L	Mosaic	Inlay	Geometric design	$300.
1638	1.0L	Mosaic	Inlay	Geometric design	$200.

1568 6.0L, 1632 5.0L

Number	Size	Type	Lid	Description	Value
1641	.5L	Tapestry	Pewter	Cavalier with pipe and jug of wine	$275.
1641	1.0L	Tapestry	Pewter		$325.
1642	.5L	Tapestry	Pewter	Man drinking	$275.
1642	1.0L	Tapestry	Pewter		$325.
1643	.5L	Tapestry	Pewter	Student drinking	$275.
1643	1.0L	Tapestry	Pewter		$325.
1644	.5L	Tapestry	Pewter	Man smoking	$275.
1644	1.0L	Tapestry	Pewter		$325.

1533 .5L, 1641 .5L, 1645 .5L

Number	Size	Type	Lid	Description	Value
1645	.5L	Tapestry	Pewter	Man with guitar and stein	$275.
1645	1.0L	Tapestry	Pewter		$325.
1646	.5L	Tapestry	Pewter	Man drinking	$275.
1646	1.0L	Tapestry	Pewter		$325.
1647	.5L	Tapestry	Pewter	Peasant holding stein aloft	$275.
1647	1.0L	Tapestry	Pewter		$325.
1648	.5L	Tapestry	Pewter	Man holding open stein	$275.
1648	1.0L	Tapestry	Pewter		$325.

1642 1.0L, 1643 1.0L, 1662 1.0L

Number	Size	Type	Lid	Description	Value
1649	1.0L	Tapestry	Pewter	Full figure of man with sign	$350.
1650	1.0L	Tapestry	Pewter	Mountaineer	$375.
1654	.25L	Mosaic	Inlay	Geometric design	$225.
1654	.5L	Mosaic	Inlay	Geometric design	$275.
1655	.5L	Etched	Inlay	Young people dancing (mate to 1656)	$525.
1656	.5L	Etched	Inlay	Old people dancing (mate to 1655)	$525.
1662	.5L	Tapestry	Pewter	Blacksmith	$300.
1662	1.0L	Tapestry	Pewter		$350.

1675 .5L   1687 .5L   1698 .5L

Number	Size	Type	Lid	Description	Value
1675	.5L	Etched	Inlay	Scene of Heidelberg, years *1386 to 1886* on medallion at rear of some steins	$550.
1687	.5L	Relief	Inlay	Barrel shape	$250.
1690	4.5L	Etched	Inlay	Man and woman riding horses, signed Warth (master to 1695)	$2200.
1695	.5L	Etched	Inlay	Four panels, hunters (master is 1690)	$675.
1698	.5L	Tapestry	Pewter	Old building	$300.
1713	2.0L	Relief	None	Geometric design	$325.
1720	2.0L	Relief	None	Geometric design	$375.
1723	.5L	Etched	Inlay	Scene at town of Mettlach, signed Warth	$1250.

1695 .5L, 1724 .5L, 1733 .5L

Number	Size	Type	Lid	Description	Value
1724	.5L	Etched	Inlay	Fireman stein, fireman's hat on inlay, signed Warth	$1600.
1725	.25L	Etched	Inlay	Lovers, man holding stein, signed Warth (master is 1734)	$350.
1725	.5L	Etched	Inlay		$550.
1726	1.5L	Mosaic	Inlay	Geometric design, pitcher shape	$275.

1725 .5L, 1732 .5L

Number	Size	Type	Lid	Description	Value
1727	.25L	Relief	Inlay	Leaves and scrolls	$160.
1727	.5L	Relief	Inlay		$200.
1732	.5L	Etched	Inlay	Prussian eagle and two soldiers	$900.
1733	.5L	Etched	Inlay	Jockey stein, jockey on horse, jockey's cap on inlay, signed Warth	$1250.
1734	1.4L	Etched	Inlay	Lovers, man holding glass aloft, jeweled base, signed Warth (master to 1725, matches pokal 1735)	$1150.
1734	2.1L	Etched	Inlay		$1150.
1736	3.0L	Relief	Inlay	Four panels with man in each, relief in full color (master to set 1756 to 1759)	$450.

1736 3.0L, 1756 1.0L

1757 1.0L, 1758 1.0L, 1786 .5L

Number	Size	Type	Lid	Description	Value
1736	3.0L	Relief	Inlay	Relief not in full color	$375.
1737	2.0L	Relief	Inlay	Wheat design	$275.
1738	3.0L	Mosaic	Inlay	Wheat design (master to 1744)	$325.
1739	3.3L	Relief	Inlay	Coat of arms, men on either side	$550.
—1740	.25L	Relief	Inlay	Floral design	$150.—
1741	.5L	Etched	Inlay	Scene of Tubingen, signed Warth	$550.
1742	.5L	Etched	Inlay	Scene of Gottingen	$550.
1744	.3L	Mosaic	Inlay	Wheat design (master is 1738)	$160.
1745	.25L	Relief	Inlay	Leaves and scroll design	$160.
1750	1.0L	Mosaic	Inlay	Geometric design, pitcher shape	$300.

Set of Four

Number	Size	Type	Lid	Description	Value
1756	1.0L	Relief & Tapestry	Inlay	Man drinking, relief in full color	$400.
1757	1.0L	Relief & Tapestry	Inlay	Man wearing a bib, relief in full color	$400.
1758	1.0L	Relief & Tapestry	Inlay	Soldier, relief in full color	$400.
1759	1.0L	Relief & Tapestry	Inlay	Old man with a pipe, relief in full color (master to set is 1736)	$400.
1771	3.0L	Mosaic	Inlay	Geometric design	$475.

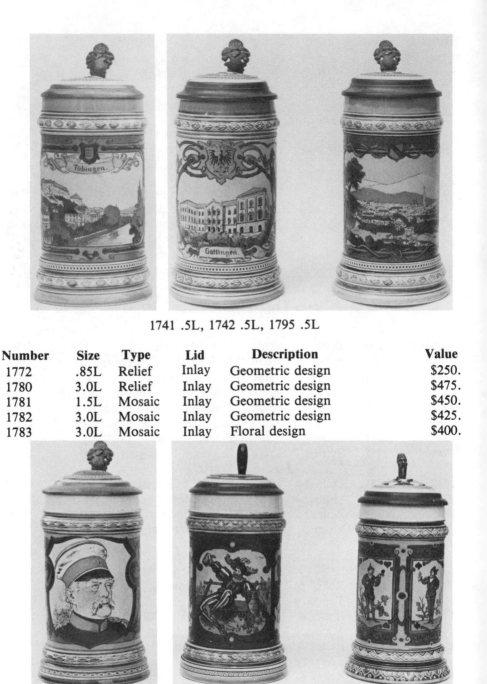

1741 .5L, 1742 .5L, 1795 .5L

Number	Size	Type	Lid	Description	Value
1772	.85L	Relief	Inlay	Geometric design	$250.
1780	3.0L	Relief	Inlay	Geometric design	$475.
1781	1.5L	Mosaic	Inlay	Geometric design	$450.
1782	3.0L	Mosaic	Inlay	Geometric design	$425.
1783	3.0L	Mosaic	Inlay	Floral design	$400.

1794 .5L, 1796 .5L, 1797 .5L

Number	Size	Type	Lid	Description	Value
1786	.5L	Etched	Pewter	St. Florian putting out fire, handle is dragon, thumblift is ceramic dragon's head, lid looks like tiled roof	$675.
1786	1.0L	Etched	Pewter		$975.
1786	.5L	Etched	Pewter	Lid is relief scene of Munich	$725.
1786	1.0L	Etched	Pewter	Lid has tiered steeple shape with pewter dragon's head thumblift	$975.
1787	.5L	Mosaic	Inlay	Geometric design	$275.
1788	.5L	Mosaic	Inlay	Geometric design	$325.
1789	.3L	Mosaic	Inlay	Floral design	$275.
1789	.5L	Mosaic	Inlay		$350.
1790	.5L	Mosaic	Inlay	Geometric design	$200.
1791	2.75L	Relief	Inlay	Floral design and gargoyles	$300.

1802 .5L, 1803 .25L, 1809 .5L

Number	Size	Type	Lid	Description	Value
1794	.5L	Etched	Inlay	Bismarck in uniform, signed Warth	$450.
1795	.5L	Etched	Inlay	Scene of Freiburg, signed Warth	$550.
1796	.5L	Etched	Inlay	Cavalier drinking, signed Warth	$500.
1797	.5L	Etched	Inlay	Four cards, gold coins on lid	$675.
1799	.5L	Etched	Inlay	Faces in medallions	$475.
1800	3.0L	Mosaic	None	Geometric design	$325.

1817 3.1L, 1851 3.2L   1822 3.0L

Number	Size	Type	Lid	Description	Value
1801	.3L	Mosaic	Inlay	Geometric design	$250.
1802	.5L	Mosaic	Inlay	Floral design	$225.
1803	.25L	Mosaic	Inlay	Geometric design	$250.
1809	.5L	Etched & Relief	Inlay	Five panels, one figure in each, in full color relief (matches pokal 1820)	$550.
1809	1.0L	Etched & Relief	Inlay		$850.
1815	4.0L	Mosaic	Inlay	Floral design (master to 1816)	$475.
1816	.5L	Mosaic & Relief	Inlay	Floral design (master is 1815)	$300.
1817	3.1L	Etched	Pewter	Man with high wheel bicycle, signed Schultz (mate to 1851)	$2500.
1818	6.2L	Etched	Pewter	Tavern scene, signed Gorig	$1800.
1819	.5L	Etched	Inlay	Masonic stein, signed Warth	$950.
1821	3.2L	Relief	Inlay	Musician with guitar	$350.

Number	Size	Type	Lid	Description	Value
1822	3.0L	Mosaic	Inlay	Floral design	$400.
1823	.5L	Etched	Inlay	Bird in flight and hunters with dogs, signed Hein (mate to 1453)	$575.
1827	3.0L	Mosaic	Inlay	Geometric design	$375.
1830	3.0L	Etched	Inlay	Four panels with men in each panel, signed Warth	$1600.
1831	3.0L	Mosaic	Inlay	Floral design	$350.
1832	3.0L	Relief	Inlay	Geometric design	$400.
1837	.3L	Mosaic	Pewter	Floral design	$150.
1850	.3L	Mosaic	Inlay	Geometric design	$250.
1851	3.2L	Etched	Pewter	4F stein, athletic scenes, signed Schultz (mate to 1817)	$2800.
1852	3.0L	PUG	Pewter	Print under glaze blank body (see PUG Steins)	—

1830 3.0L

1818 6.2L

Number	Size	Type	Lid	Description	Value
1854	3.0L	Relief	Inlay	Geometric design	$400.
1855	.5L	PUG	Pewter	Print under glaze blank body (see PUG steins)	—
1856	.5L	Etched & Glazed	Inlay	Postman stein, black eagle on a blue body (mate to 2075)	$1600.
1856	1.0L	Etched & Glazed	Inlay		$2100.
			Set of Three		
1861	.5L	Etched & PUG	Inlay	Frederick III	$375.
1861	.5L	Etched & PUG	Inlay	Wilhelm I	$375.
1861	.5L	Etched & PUG	Inlay	Wilhelm II	$375.
1861	.5L	Etched & PUG	Pewter	*Gambrinus Rex*	$325.
1863	.5L	Etched	Inlay	Scene of Stuttgart	$575.
1864	4.5L	Etched	Pewter	*Hipp Hipp Hurrah,* oarsman with rowing equipment	$2000.
1868	1.5L	Mosaic	None	Floral design	$350.
1872	2.0L	Relief	Inlay	Two panels of figures	$350.
1878	2.0L	Mosaic	Inlay	Geometric design	$350.
1890	.5L	Etched & PUG	Inlay	Wilhelm, I, Wilhelm II, and Frederick III	$425.

1856 .5L, 1863 .5L, 1861 Wilhelm II .5L

1819 .5L, 1890 .5L, 1893 1.0L

Number	Size	Type	Lid	Description	Value
1892	1.0L	Mosaic	Pewter	Floral design, shape and lid resemble faience	$375.
1893	1.0L	Mosaic	Pewter	Geometric design, shape and lid resemble faience	$400.
1894	.25L	Relief	Inlay	Faces and leaves	$140.
1894	.5L	Relief	Inlay		$170.
1896	.25L	Relief	Inlay	Figures	$160.
1901	.3L	Mosaic	Inlay	Geometric design	$200.
1902	2.0L	Mosaic	Pewter	Geometric design	$375.
1905	2.0L	Mosaic	Inlay	Geometric design (master to 1906)	$475.
1906	.25L	Mosaic	Inlay	Geometric design (master is 1905)	$250.
1908	1.0L	PUG	Pewter	Print under glaze blank body (see PUG Steins)	—
1909	.25L	PUG	Pewter	Print under glaze blank body (see PUG Steins)	—
1909	.3L	PUG	Pewter		—
1909	.4L	PUG	Pewter		—
1909	.5L	PUG	Pewter		—
1912	2.4L	Mosaic	Inlay	Floral design (master to 1917)	$400.
1914	.5L	Etched	Inlay	4F stein, man holding flag and dumbbell	$700.

1915 Trier .5L, 1915 Cologne .5L, 1914 .5L

Number	Size	Type	Lid	Description	Value
1915	.5L	Etched & PUG	Inlay	Trier Cathedral, signed Warth and Martin	$550.
1915	.5L	Etched & PUG	Inlay	Cologne Cathedral, signed Warth	$550.
1915	.5L	Etched	Inlay	Cologne Cathedral, signed Warth	$600.
1916	2.15L	Etched	Inlay	Cavaliers drinking, signed Warth (same scene as 1932)	$1400.
1917	.25L	Mosaic	Inlay	Floral design (master is 1912)	$225.
1918	2.0L	Mosaic	Inlay	Floral design (master to 1919)	$475.
1919	.25L	Mosaic	Inlay	Floral design (master is 1918)	$250.
1920	2.5L	Mosaic	Pewter	Floral design	$375.
1922	2.5L	Mosaic	Inlay	Geometric design (master to 1939)	$425.
1923	.25L	Relief	Inlay	Scrolls and medallions	$170.
1926	2.0L	Relief	Pewter	Verse	$225.
1927	1.0L	Relief	Pewter	Verse	$140.
1927	1.5L	Relief	Pewter		$150.
1927	2.0L	Relief	Pewter		$200.
1928	1.0L	Relief	Pewter	Geometric design	$150.
1928	1.5L	Relief	Pewter		$175.
1928	2.0L	Relief	Pewter		$225.
1929	1.5L	Mosaic	Pewter	Geometric design	$400.

Number	Size	Type	Lid	Description	Value
1932	.5L	Etched	Inlay	Cavaliers drinking, signed Warth (same scene as 1916)	$525.
1932	1.0L	Etched	Inlay		$675.
1934	.5L	Etched	Inlay	Four panels of soldiers, uniforms from 1689, 1757, 1813, and 1889	$900.
1938	.25L	Mosaic	Inlay	Geometric design	$225.
1939	.25L	Mosaic	Inlay	Geometric design (master is 1922)	$225.
1940	3.0L	Relief	Pewter	Yale University emblem	$450.
1940	3.0L	Etched	Inlay	Keeper of wine cellar, signed Warth (same scene as 1941)	$1250.
1941	3.0L	Etched	Pewter	Keeper of wine cellar, signed Warth (same scene as 1940)	$1200.
1945	2.0L	Relief	Inlay	Leaf and scroll design	$400.
1946	.5L	Etched	Inlay	Courting scene	$525.
1947	.5L	Etched	Inlay	Man and verse	$500.

1940 Yale University 3.0L, 1940 3.0L, 1941 3.0L

Number	Size	Type	Lid	Description	Value
1949	3.0L	Etched	Inlay	Two lovers, stork with baby, and stork with rings (master to 1968)	$975.
1950	3.0L	Etched	Inlay	Prussian eagle, overlay bust of Wilhelm I, jeweled base, crown on inlay (same scene as 1956)	$3000.
1951	2.3L	Etched	Inlay	Four seasons in four panels (masters to 1972)	$1000.
1952	3.0L	Mosaic	Inlay	Floral design	$350.
1953	2.5L	Mosaic	Inlay	Floral design	$400.
1954	2.0L	Mosaic	Inlay	Geometric design	$350.
1956	1.0L	Etched	Inlay	Prussian eagle, overlay bust of Wilhelm I (similar to 2204, same scene as 1950)	$2500.
1962	3.0L	Mosaic	Inlay	Geometric design (master to 1963)	$400.
1963	.25L	Mosaic	Inlay	Geometric design (master is 1962)	$225.
1964	2.0L	Mosaic	Inlay	Geometric design (master to 1965)	$450.
1965	.3L	Mosaic	Inlay	Geometric design (master is 1964)	$200.

1932 .5L, 1934 .5L, 1956 1.0L

1946 .5L, 1947 .5L, 1976 .4L

Number	Size	Type	Lid	Description	Value
1968	.25L	Etched	Inlay	Two lovers (master is 1949)	$300.
1968	.5L	Etched	Inlay		$475.
1970	3.0L	Mosaic	Inlay	Floral design	$475.
1972	.25L	Etched	Inlay	Four seasons in four panels (master is 1951)	$350.
1972	.5L	Etched	Inlay		$525.
1973	2.5L	Mosaic	Inlay	Geometric design (master to 1974)	$375.
1974	.3L	Relief	Inlay	Geometric design (master is 1973)	$200.
1975	.4L	Etched	Inlay	Ram	$500.
1976	.4L	Etched	Inlay	Verse	$300.
1977	.5L	Mosaic	Inlay	Floral design	$325.
1979	.3L	Mosaic	Inlay	Geometric design	$225.
1980	.3L	Mosaic	Inlay	Geometric design	$225.
1983	.25L	Mosaic	Inlay	Geometric design (master is 1984)	$300.
1983	.5L	Mosaic	Inlay		$375.
1984	3.4L	Mosaic	Inlay	Geometric design (master to 1983)	$500.
1985	3.0L	Mosaic	None	Floral design	$375.
1986	.5L	Etched	Inlay	Two ladies, signed Warth (master is 1161)	$550.
1987	.25L	Etched	Inlay	Wild rose design	$275.
1987	.5L	Etched	Inlay		$375.

1938 .25L

1968 .5L

1972 .5L

Number	Size	Type	Lid	Description	Value
1989	1.5L	Relief	Inlay	Geometric design	$350.
1990	2.5L	Mosaic	Inlay	Geometric design (master to 1993)	$450.
1992	2.0L	Mosaic	Inlay	Floral design (master to 1994)	$425.

1984 3.4L

1951 2.3L

1963 .25L, 1975 .4L, 1983 .5L

Number	Size	Type	Lid	Description	Value
1993	.3L	Mosaic	Inlay	Geometric design (master is 1990)	$275.
1994	.25L	Mosaic	Inlay	Floral design (master is 1992)	$275.
1995	.5L	Etched	Inlay	Fat man drinking	$475.
1996	.5L	PUG	Pewter	Print under glaze blank body (see PUG Steins)	—
1997	.5L	Etched & PUG	Inlay	George Ehret brewer	$275.
1998	.5L	Etched	Inlay	*Trumpeter from Sackingen* (master is 1562)	$500.

1986 .5L, 1995 .5L, 1998 .5L

1997 .5L, 1998 Martin Moehn .5L, 1999 .5L

Number	Size	Type	Lid	Description	Value
1998	.5L	Etched & PUG	Inlay	Martin Moehn Brewery	$600.
1999	.5L	Etched	Inlay	Three scenes, men drinking	$475.

2002 1.0L, 2003 .5L, 2005 .5L

Number	Size	Type	Lid	Description	Value
				Set of Eleven	
2001A	.5L	Etched & Glazed	Inlay	Book stein for law	$475.
2001B	.5L	Etched & Glazed	Inlay	Book stein for medicine	$475.
2001C	.5L	Etched & Glazed	Inlay	Book stein for scholars	$550.
2001D	.5L	Etched & Glazed	Inlay	Book stein for mathematics	$550.
2001E	.5L	Etched & Glazed	Inlay	Book stein for natural science	$650.
2001F	.5L	Etched & Glazed	Inlay	Book stein for architecture	$550.

2001B .5L, 2001K .5L, 2001 Cornell University .5L

Number	Size	Type	Lid	Description	Value
2001G	.5L	Etched & Glazed	Inlay	Book stein for engineering	$650.
2001H	.5L	Etched & Glazed	Inlay	Book stein for forestry	$650.
2001I	.5L	Etched & Glazed	Inlay	Book stein for theology	$650.
2001K	.5L	Etched & Glazed	Inlay	Book stein for banking or commerce	$475.
2001L	.5L	Etched & Glazed	Inlay	Book stein for mining or mountaineering	$650.
2001	.5L	Etched & Glazed	Inlay	Book stein for Cornell University	$1600.
2002	.5L	Etched	Inlay	Munich stein, town of Munich	$450.
2002	1.0L	Etched	Inlay		$625.

Number	Size	Type	Lid	Description	Value
2003	.5L	Etched	Inlay	Three panels: troubadour, knight with stein, and knight with pokal (matches pokal 1785)	$525.
2004	.4L	Etched	Inlay	Wolfhound on the side, handle is its tail	$1500.
2004	.5L	Etched	Inlay		$1700.
2005	.5L	Etched	Inlay	Four people having dinner, signed H.D.	$475.
2006	.5L	Etched	Inlay	Lovers and garlands, signed Hein	$550.
				Set of Three	
2007	.5L	Etched	Inlay	Black cat stein, *Hidigeigei,* signed Stuck	$600.
2008	.5L	Etched	Inlay	Trumpeter on black horse, signed Stuck	$550.
2009	.5L	Etched	Inlay	Werner and Margarete dancing, signed Stuck, these scenes are from *Trumpeter from Sackingen*	$550.
2012	.25L	Mosaic	Inlay	Art nouveau, unusual shape, geometric design	$300.
2012	.5L	Mosaic	Inlay		$400.
2015	5.6L	Relief	Pewter	St. George and the dragon, relief in full color (master to 2016)	$1800.

2007 .5L, 2008 .5L, 2009 .5L

2004 .5L pewter lid:
value $1250.

2024 .5L, 3043 .5L

Number	Size	Type	Lid	Description	Value
2016	.3L	Relief	Pewter	Shield design (master is 2015)	$225.
2018	.5L	Character	Stoneware	Pug dog	$975.
2019	1.0L	PUG	Pewter	Print under glaze blank body (see PUG Steins)	—
2019	1.5L	PUG	Pewter		—
2019	2.0L	PUG	Pewter		—
2019	3.0L	PUG	Pewter		—
2020	2.0L	Mosaic	Inlay	Floral design	$450.
2024	.5L	Etched & Glazed	Inlay	Berlin stein, shield of Berlin (mate to 3043)	$700.
2025	.3L	Etched	Inlay	Cherubs carousing	$300.
2025	.5L	Etched	Inlay		$450.
2027	.5L	Etched	Inlay	Gambrinus	$900.
2027	1.0L	Etched	Inlay		$1300.
2028	.5L	Etched	Inlay	Tavern scene, ten men drinking and tavern keeper filling steins	$500.
2028	1.0L	Etched	Inlay		$650.

2029 .5L, 2030 .5L, 2031 .5L

Number	Size	Type	Lid	Description	Value
				Set of Three	
2029	.5L	Etched	Inlay	Target in front, soldiers on sides	$950.
2030	.5L	Etched	Inlay	Soldiers drinking	$950.
2031	.5L	Etched	Inlay	Officers and soldiers	$950.

2027 .5L, 2028 1.0L, 2033 1.0L

2012 .25L, 2034 .5L, 2043 .4L

Number	Size	Type	Lid	Description	Value
2033	.5L	Etched & Glazed	Inlay	Oak and two deer, *Westerwaid* style	$700.
2033	1.0L	Etched & Glazed	Inlay		$900.
2034	.5L	Mosaic	Inlay	Geometric design	$400.
2035	.3L	Etched	Inlay	*Bacchus* carousing (mate to 2057, matches loving cup 2167)	$300.
2035	.5L	Etched	Inlay		$450.
2035	1.0L	Etched	Inlay		$575.
2036	.5L	Character	Stoneware	Owl, signed Hein	$950.

2025 .5L, 2035 .5L, 2057 .5L

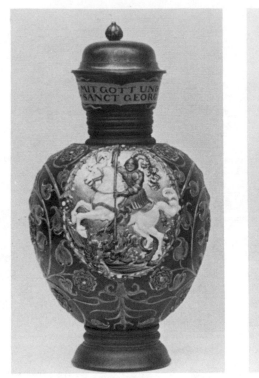

2015 5.6L

2038 3.8L

2049 .5L, 2050 .5L, 2051 .5L

Number	Size	Type	Lid	Description	Value
2038	3.8L	Etched & Relief	Inlay	Town of Rodenstein, houses and towers on inlay, relief is in full color, frequently incorrectly called *The Black Forest* stein (master to 2829 and mate to 2824)	$4000.
2040	4.1L	Etched	Inlay	German soldiers, ca. 1890, helmet on inlay	$7500.
2040	4.1L	Etched	Pewter		$4500.
2043	.4L	Mosaic	Inlay	Unusual shape, windows in middle of stein, flowers on the windows	$500.
2044	.5L	Etched	Inlay	Drinking scene	$650.
2049	.5L	Etched	Inlay	Chess stein, chessboard	$2000.
2050	.5L	Etched	Inlay	Slipper stein, man and woman, slipper on inlay	$1250.
2051	.5L	Etched	Inlay	Seven students drinking	$600.

2064 2.25L

2053 3.5L

2040 4.1L

2044 .5L, 2068 .5L, 2074 .5L

Number	Size	Type	Lid	Description	Value
2052	.25L	Etched	Inlay	Munich Child	$400.
2053	3.5L	Etched	Inlay	4F motif, monkeys all around stein	$3500.
2054	.5L	Etched	Inlay	Cavalier leaning on a barrel	$500.
2056	2.0L	Relief & Mosaic	Pewter	Barley and hops design, gargoyle on spout, ewer shape (master to 2067)	$500.

2018 .5L, 2036 .5L, 2069 .5L

Number	Size	Type	Lid	Description	Value
2057	.3L	Etched	Inlay	Peasants dancing (mate to 2035)	$300.
2057	.5L	Etched	Inlay		$450.
2064	2.25L	Etched & Relief	Inlay	Young boy bowling, relief in full color	$1800.
2065	1.5L	Etched	Inlay	Man and barmaid, jeweled base, signed Schlitt (master to 2230, matches pokal 2066)	$1150.
2065	2.4L	Etched	Inlay		$1150.
2067	.5L	Relief & Mosaic	Inlay	Barley and hops design (master is 2056)	$325.
2068	.5L	Etched	Inlay	Drinking scene	$575.

2075 .5L, 2082 .5L, 2083 .5L

Number	Size	Type	Lid	Description	Value
2069	.5L	Character	Stone-ware	Monkey	$1600.
2074	.5L	Etched	Inlay	*Bird in the cage* stein, lonely drinker	$1500.
2075	.5L	Etched & Glazed	Inlay	Telegrapher stein, large black eagle on a blue body (mate to 1856)	$1600.
2076	1.85L	Relief	Inlay	Coat of arms (master to 2077)	$250.
2076	3.2L	Relief	Inlay		$300.
2077	.3L	Relief	Inlay	Coat of arms (master is 2076)	$150.
2077	.5L	Relief	Inlay		$185.

Number	Size	Type	Lid	Description	Value
2082	.3L	Etched	Inlay	William Tell stein, shooting apple off his son's head (mate to 2083)	$1350.
2082	.5L	Etched	Inlay		$1350.
2082	1.0L	Etched	Inlay		$2100.
2083	.3L	Etched	Inlay	Boar hunt stein, (mate to 2082, these .3L have large false bottoms, they are the same heights as .5L)	$1350.
2083	.5L	Etched	Inlay		$1350.
2083	1.0L	Etched	Inlay		$2100.
2085	4.15L	Relief	Inlay	Dancing scene (master to 2086, matches punch bowl 2087)	$350.
2086	.25L	Relief	Inlay	Dancing scene (master is 2085,	$160.
2086	.5L	Relief	Inlay	matches punch bowl 2087)	$200.
			Set of Four		
2089	.5L	Etched	Inlay	Angel serving dinner and beer to gentleman, signed Schlitt	$650.
2090	.3L	Etched	Inlay	Club stein, man at table in his club smoking pipe, signed Schlitt	$450.
2090	.5L	Etched	Inlay		$550.
2090	1.0L	Etched	Inlay		$675.
2091	.5L	Etched	Inlay	St. Florian pouring water on a man's head, by Schlitt	$850.

2089 .5L, 2090 .5L, 2091 .5L

2092 .5L, 2093 .5L, 2094 .5L

Number	Size	Type	Lid	Description	Value
2092	.5L	Etched	Inlay	Keeper of clock tower, gnome on ladder setting clock, signed Schlitt	$650.
2093	.5L	Etched	Inlay	Card stein, four cards around bulbous body	$700.
2094	.5L	Etched	Inlay	Lady playing fiddle, dancers	$550.
2095	2.5L	Etched	Inlay	Drinking Germans and Romans, row of medallions around base of stein, signed Schlitt	$2500.
2095	2.5L	Etched	Inlay	Same scene, but with raised flowers wrapped around body of stein	$2800.
2096	2.0L	Etched	Inlay	Fancy dandy with hat	$2300.
2097	.5L	Etched	Inlay	Musical notes	$500.
2098	4.4L	Mosaic	Inlay	Floral design (master to 2099)	$475.
2099	.4L	Mosaic	Inlay	Floral design (master is 2098)	$275.
2100	.3L	Etched	Inlay	*Prosit* stein, knight with stein and man with fur clothing, signed Schlitt	$600.
2100	.5L	Etched	Inlay		$900.
2101	.5L	Etched	Inlay	Man carrying stein and boar's head on tray, inlay resembles a rooftop	$550.
2102	5.75L	Etched	Pewter	*Germania* stein, coats of arms around stein, signed Schultz	$5000.

2097 .5L, 2100 .5L, 2106 .5L

2076 3.2L, 2085 4.15L

2095 2.5L   2096 2.0L   2102 5.75L

Number	Size	Type	Lid	Description	Value
2103	1.5L	Etched	Inlay	Man sitting on barrel and drinking beer, jeweled base (same scene as 1494, mate to 2104 and 2105)	$950.
2104	1.5L	Etched	Inlay	Cavalier leaning on staff, jeweled base (same scene as 1498, mate to 2103 and 2105)	$950.
2105	1.5L	Etched	Inlay	*Trumpeter of Sackingen,* jeweled base (same scene as 1562, mate to 2103 and 2104)	$950.

Number	Size	Type	Lid	Description	Value
2106	.4L	Etched & Relief	Inlay	Monkeys in cage, monkey handle	$1600.
2107	1.5L	Etched	Inlay	*Gambrinus* on throne, jeweled base, signed Schlitt (matches pokal 2110)	$1350.
2107	2.25L	Etched	Inlay		$1350.
2118	1.0L	PUG	Pewter	Print under glaze blank body (see PUG Steins)	—
2118	1.5L	PUG	Pewter		—
2118	2.0L	PUG	Pewter		—
2118	3.0L	PUG	Pewter		—

2103 1.5L, 2105 1.5L, 2104 1.5L

Number	Size	Type	Lid	Description	Value
2121	.25L	Etched	Inlay	Young children playing	$375.
2122	3.8L	Etched	Inlay	Crusader stein, crusaders drinking, signed Schlitt	$3400.
2123	.3L	Etched	Inlay	Drinking knight stein, signed Schlitt	$600.
2123	.5L	Etched	Inlay		$1300.
2124	3.0L	Relief	Inlay	Birds in flight (master to 2125)	$425.
2125	.25L	Relief	Inlay	Bird in flight (master is 2124)	$200.

2123 .5L   2131 .5L Relief, 2131 .5L Cameo

1734 2.1L, 2065 2.4L, 2107 1.5L

2126 5.5L, 2122 3.8L

Number	Size	Type	Lid	Description	Value
2126	5.5L	Etched	Pewter	*Symphonia* stein, composers around stein, signed Schultz	$4200.
2128	2.0L	Relief	Inlay	Floral and geometric design	$375.
2130	.5L	Relief	Inlay	Man drinking (matches pokal 2132)	$250.
2130	.5L	Cameo	Inlay	Man drinking	$675.
2131	.5L	Relief	Inlay	Barroom characters	$250.
2131	1.0L	Relief	Inlay		$325.

Number	Size	Type	Lid	Description	Value
2133	.5L	Etched	Inlay	Gnome in tree, drinking from goblet, by Schlitt (mate to 2134, matches plaque 2113)	$1600.
2134	.3L	Etched	Inlay	Gnome in nest, holding two steins, by Schlitt (mate to 2133 matches plaque 2112)	$800.
2134	.5L	Etched	Inlay		$1600.
2136	.5L	Etched & PUG	Inlay	Anheuser Busch Brewery	$750.
2140	.5L	PUG	Pewter	Print under glaze blank body (see PUG Steins)	—
2176	2.7L	PUG	Pewter	Print under glaze blank body (see PUG Steins)	—
2177	.25L	PUG	Pewter	Print under glaze blank body (see PUG Steins)	—
2178	2.5L	PUG	Pewter	Print under glaze blank body (see PUG Steins)	—
2179	.25L	PUG	Pewter	Print under glaze blank body (see PUG Steins)	—
2180	3.3L	PUG	Pewter	Print under glaze blank body (see PUG Steins)	—
2181	.25L	PUG	Pewter	Print under glaze blank body (see PUG Steins)	—
2182	.5L	Relief	Inlay	Bowling scene	$275.

2133 .5L, 2134 .5L, 2136 .5L

Number	Size	Type	Lid	Description	Value
2183	3.25L	PUG	Inlay	Print under glaze blank body (see PUG Steins)	—
2184	.3L	PUG	Inlay	Print under glaze blank body (see PUG Steins)	—
2184	.5L	PUG	Inlay		—
2185	.5L	Etched	Inlay	People in fancy clothes	$550.
2186	.5L	Relief	Inlay	Cavalier on front	$300.
2189	.25L	PUG	Pewter	Print under glaze blank body (see PUG Steins)	—
2190	.5L	Etched	Inlay	Bicycle scene with seven bicycles	$800.
2191	.5L	Etched	Inlay	Military joke, Etruscan style, signed Schlitt (mate to 2192)	$1050.
2192	.5L	Etched	Inlay	Student joke, Etruscan style, signed Schlitt (mate to 2191)	$900.
2193	3.0L	Etched	Pewter	Soldiers and maidens at tavern, Etruscan style, signed Schlitt	$1800.
2194	3.3L	Relief	Inlay	*In the whale at Ascalon,* alligator handle (master to 2243 through 2245 and 2363)	$700.
2201	4.15L	Etched	Inlay	*Xantippe and Socrates,* Etruscan style, by Schlitt (mate to 2383)	$3400.

2121 .25L, 2182 .5L, 2185 .5L

2190 .5L, 2191 .5L, 2192 .5L

2204 1.0L

2193 3.0L

2201 4.15L, 2223 5.5L

Number	Size	Type	Lid	Description	Value
2204	.5L	Etched	Inlay	Blue Max stein, Prussian eagle on tan body	$500.
2204	1.0L	Etched	Inlay		$950.
2205	5.2L	Etched	Inlay	Hunters and Diana after hunt at tavern, squirrel on inlay	$2500.
2206	3.0L	Etched	Inlay	Tavern scene	$1200.
2210	3.25L	Relief	Inlay	Tavern and bowling scene (master to 2211)	$325.
2210	3.25L	Cameo	Inlay		$650.
2211	.3L	Relief	Inlay	Tavern and bowling scene (master is 2210)	$165.

Number	Size	Type	Lid	Description	Value
2214	3.0L	Hand Painted	Pewter	Fraternal crest	$500.
2219	3.15L	Relief	Inlay	Dancing and musical scenes, three panels (master to 2246 through 2248)	$500.
2220	3.8L	Relief	Inlay	Geometric design and bird (master to 2232)	$550.
2222	.5L	PUG	Inlay	Print under glaze blank body (see PUG Steins)	—
2223	5.5L	Etched	Pewter	Tavern scene	$2300.
2227	4.35L	PUG	Inlay	Print under glaze blank body (see PUG Stein)	—
2230	.5L	Etched	Inlay	Man and barmaid, by Schlitt (master is 2065)	$550.
2231	.5L	Etched	Inlay	Tavern scene	$550.
2232	.3L	Relief	Inlay	Geometric design and bird (master is 2220)	$175.

2205 5.2L, 2206 3.0L   2214 3.0L

Number	Size	Type	Lid	Description	Value
2235	.5L	Etched	Inlay	Barmaid holding steins, target in background	$600.
2235	1.0L	Etched	Inlay		$900.
2238	.5L	Etched	Inlay	7th Regt. Armory stein, eagle and flags	$1200.

2219 3.15L, 2220 3.8L

Number	Size	Type	Lid	Description	Value
			Set of Three		
2243	.3L	Relief	Inlay	*In the whale at Ascalon* (master is 2194)	$190.
2244	.3L	Relief	Inlay	*In the whale at Ascalon* (master is 2194)	$190.
2245	.3L	Relief	Inlay	*In the whale at Ascalon* (master is 2194)	$190.

2243 .3L, 2247 .3L, 2250 .3L

Number	Size	Type	Lid	Description	Value
			Set of Three		
2246	.3L	Relief	Inlay	Peasants dancing (master is 2219)	$180.
2247	.3L	Relief	Inlay	Peasants dancing (master is 2219)	$180.
2248	.3L	Relief	Inlay	Peasants dancing (master is 2219)	$180.

2230 .5L, 2231 .5L, 2235 .5L

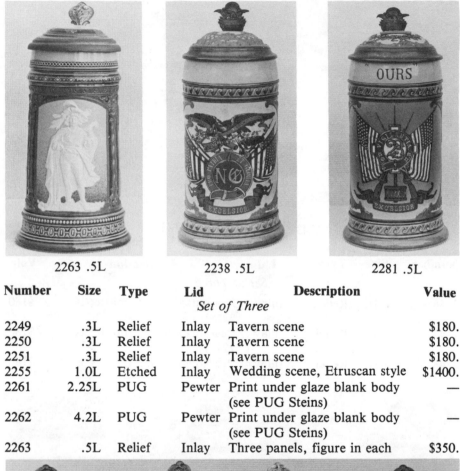

2263 .5L   2238 .5L   2281 .5L

Number	Size	Type	Lid	Description	Value
				Set of Three	
2249	.3L	Relief	Inlay	Tavern scene	$180.
2250	.3L	Relief	Inlay	Tavern scene	$180.
2251	.3L	Relief	Inlay	Tavern scene	$180.
2255	1.0L	Etched	Inlay	Wedding scene, Etruscan style	$1400.
2261	2.25L	PUG	Pewter	Print under glaze blank body (see PUG Steins)	—
2262	4.2L	PUG	Pewter	Print under glaze blank body (see PUG Steins)	—
2263	.5L	Relief	Inlay	Three panels, figure in each	$350.

2276 .25L, 2277 Heidelberg .3L, 2227 Nurnberg .3L, 2227 Wartburg .25L

Number	Size	Type	Lid	Description	Value
2270	3.3L	PUG	Pewter	Print under glaze blank body (see PUG Steins)	—
2271	.5L	PUG	Pewter	Print under glaze blank body (see PUG Steins)	—
2276	.25L	Etched & Relief	Inlay	Nurnberg goose boy, full color relief	$350.
2276	.5L	Etched & Relief	Inlay		$550.

2255 1.0L, 2282 .5L, 2285 .5L

Number	Size	Type	Lid	Description	Value
2277	.25L	Etched	Inlay	Scene at Wartburg	$350.
2277	.3L	Etched	Inlay		$350.
2277	.25L	Etched	Inlay	Scene at Heidelberg	$325.
2277	.3L	Etched	Inlay		$325.
2277	.25L	Etched	Inlay	Scene of Nurnberg	$325.
2277	.3L	Etched	Inlay		$325.
2277	.5L	Etched	Inlay		$550.
2277	.5L	Etched	Inlay	With lion and shield on inlay	$1000.
2278	.5L	Relief	Inlay	4F motif, sports scenes	$275.
2281	.5L	Etched	Inlay	23rd Regt. Armory stein, flags and rifles	$1500.

Number	Size	Type	Lid	Description	Value
2282	.5L	Etched	Inlay	Man caught drinking in beer cellar	$575.
2284	3.9L	Relief	Inlay	Drinking scenes, three panels	$600.
2285	.5L	Etched	Inlay	Guitar player and young couple	$500.
2285	1.0L	Etched	Inlay		$700.
2286	2.6L	Etched	Inlay	Tavern scene	$1100.
2300	5.5L	Etched	Pewter	Scene of Nurnberg and scenes from *Meistersinger*	$2400.
2302	.5L	Etched	Inlay	Children playing music and dancing	$550.
2303	—	PUG	Pewter	Miniature print under glaze blank body (see PUG Steins)	—

2300 5.5L

2284 3.9L

2286 2.6L

2302 .5L, 2324 .5L, 2324 .5L

Number	Size	Type	Lid	Description	Value
2324	.5L	Etched	Inlay	Early football game, football on inlay	$1600.
2324	.5L	Etched	Pewter		$900.
2332	2.7L	PUG	Pewter	Print under glaze blank body (see PUG Steins)	—
2333	.3L	PUG	Pewter	Print under glaze blank body (see PUG Steins)	—
2348	3.3L	PUG	Pewter	Print under glaze blank body (see PUG Steins)	—
2349	.3L	PUG	Pewter	Print under glaze blank body (see PUG Steins)	—
2355	4.6L	Relief	None	Mythological hunting scene, handle is young woman, signed Stahl	$950.
2356	4.6L	Relief	None	Same scene as 2355, but young man forming handle, signed Stahl	$950.
2357	4.6L	Relief	None	Same scene as 2355, but with plain handle, signed Stahl	$700.
2358	.5L	Relief	Inlay	People dining, ear of corn on inlay	$275.
2359	.3L	Relief	Inlay	Four panels with figures in each (master is 2364)	$250.

Number	Size	Type	Lid	Description	Value
2363	.5L	Relief	Inlay	*In the whale at Ascalon* (master is 2194)	$275.
2364	3.5L	Relief	Inlay	Four panels with figures in each (master to 2359)	$550.
2373	.5L	Etched	Inlay	St. Augustine, Florida, alligator handle, and its head forms thumblift	$700.
2373	.5L	Etched	None	St. Augustine, Florida, no lid, and alligator's head extends over top edge of stein	$300.
2373	.5L	Etched	Inlay	St. Augustine, Florida, plain handle	$500.
2381	3.0L	Etched	None	Two scenes of knight and maiden, ewer shape (matches plaques 2322 and 2323, and 2647 and 2648)	$1800.

2381 3.0L, 2383 4.15L

2373 .5L

Number	Size	Type	Lid	Description	Value
2382	.5L	Etched	Inlay	Thirsty rider stein or more correctly Thirsty knight stein, knight drinking in cellar, then riding off into night, conical lid, signed Schlitt	$775.
2382	1.0L	Etched	Inlay		$975.

2358 .5L, 2382 .5L, 2388 .5L

Number	Size	Type	Lid	Description	Value
2383	4.15L	Etched	Inlay	*Alexander and Diogenes,* Etruscan style, signed Schlitt (mate to 2201)	$3400.
2384	2.25L	PUG	Pewter	Print under glaze blank body (see PUG Steins)	—
2388	.5L	Character	Inlay	Pretzel stein, shaped like a pile of pretzels	$425.
2391	.5L	Etched	Inlay	*The wedding march of the Swan Knight,* or Lohengrin stein	$875.
2391	1.0L	Etched	Inlay	Larger version has castle on inlay, ornate handle and base	$2000.

2391 1.0L, 2401 1.0L

Number	Size	Type	Lid	Description	Value
2394	.5L	Etched	Inlay	Scenes from Siegfried's youth	$875.
2401	.5L	Etched	Inlay	*Tannhauser in the Venusberg*	$875.
2401	1.0L	Etched	Inlay		$1200.
2402	.5L	Etched	Inlay	*The courting of Siegfried*	$850.
2403	.5L	Etched	Inlay	Scene of Wartburg	$550.
2419	4.15L	PUG	Pewter	Print under glaze blank body (see PUG Steins)	—

2394 .5L, 2401 .5L, 2402 .5L

Number	Size	Type	Lid	Description	Value
2428	2.75L	Etched	Inlay	Tavern scene	$1150.
2430	3.0L	Etched	Inlay	Cavalier drinking	$1200.
2438	.4L	Relief	None	Plain bands around stein	$110.
2438	1.4L	Relief	None		$160.
2440	.5L	Relief & Glazed	Inlay	Figures all around stein, Capo di Monti style	$525.

2440 .5L, 2441 .5L, 2479 .5L

2455 6.8L, 2478 5.0L

Number	Size	Type	Lid	Description	Value
2441	.5L	Etched	Inlay	Gambler's stein, two dice players, by Quidenus	$700.
2448	2.5L	Cameo	None	Dancing figures, pitcher shape	$450.
2455	6.8L	Etched	Pewter	*Lohengrin's arrival*, signed Quidenus	$5800.
2478	5.0L	Cameo	Inlay	Hildebrand stein, knights on horses, swords drawn, in front of a castle, conical lid	$3600.

Number	Size	Type	Lid	Description	Value
2479	.25L	Cameo	Inlay	Hildebrand stein, three panels conical lid	$600.
2479	.5L	Cameo	Inlay		$900.
2480	.5L	Relief	Inlay	Three panels with figures, conical lid	$375.
2481	1.4L	Etched	Inlay	Hildegund aiding wounded, jeweled base	$1500.
2481	2.1L	Etched	Inlay		$1500.
2482	1.4L	Etched	Inlay	Man shooting rifle at target, jeweled base, signed Quidenus (same scene as 2599)	$1300.
2488	4.8L	PUG	Pewter	Print under glaze blank body (see PUG Steins)	—
2500	1.0L	Etched	Inlay	Wine keeper and two drunks in cellar	$800.
2501	.5L	Etched	Inlay	Scene in front of pub	$625.
2520	.5L	Etched	Inlay	Student and barmaid, signed Schlitt	$675.
2520	1.0L	Etched	Inlay		$850.

2428 2.75L, 2430 3.0L, 2481 2.1L

Number	Size	Type	Lid	Description	Value
2524	4.2L	Etched	Pewter	*Die Kannenburg* stein, knight in castle, conical lid, signed Schlitt (master to 2580, matches Beer taps 2649 and 2684)	$3400.
2525	1.6L	Relief	Pewter	Portrait, full color relief, Annaberg style	$1400.
2526	.5L	Relief	Pewter	Hunt scene, full color relief Creussen style	$1200.
2527	.25L	Relief	Pewter	Portrait, full color relief, Creussen style	$800.
2528	.5L	Etched	Inlay	Congratulating winner of bicycle race	$950.
2530	.3L	Cameo	Inlay	Boar hunt stein, signed Stahl (master is 2631)	$600.
2530	.5L	Cameo	Inlay		$850.
2530	1.0L	Cameo	Inlay		$1200.

2524 4.2L

2356 4.6L

2500 1.0L, 2520 1.0L, 2530 1.0L

2501 .5L   2525 1.6L, 2526 .5L

Number	Size	Type	Lid	Description	Value
2531	.5L	Etched	Inlay	Monk with jug of beer, signed Quidenus	$650.
2532	.5L	Etched	Inlay	Drunken scene, signed Quidenus	$550.
2547	.5L	Relief	Inlay	Loving, music making, and drinking in three panels	$275.
2547	1.0L	Relief	Inlay		$325.
2556	.5L	Relief	Inlay	Drinking scenes, three panels	$275.
2556	1.0L	Relief	Inlay		$325.
2557	.5L	Relief	Inlay	Drinking scenes, three panels	$275.
2557	1.0L	Relief	Inlay		$325.
2580	.5L	Etched	Inlay	*Die Kannenburg* stein, knight in castle, conical lid, signed Schlitt (master is 2524)	$900.
2580	1.0L	Etched	Inlay		$1400.
2581	.5L	Etched	Inlay	Musical scene with women, signed Quidenus	$550.
2582	.5L	Etched	Inlay	Jester stein, performing on table, in front of tavern, signed Quidenus	$800.
2582	1.0L	Etched	Inlay		$1000.

2580 .5L, 2581 .5L, 2582 .5L

2583 1.0L, 2585 1.0L, 2599 1.0L

Number	Size	Type	Lid	Description	Value
2583	.5L	Etched	Inlay	Egyptian stein, man orders meal, eats and drinks, then is thrown out for not paying, signed Quidenus	$1350.
2583	1.0L	Etched	Inlay		$1900.
2585	.5L	Etched & Relief	Inlay	Munich Child standing on world, full color relief	$700.
2585	1.0L	Etched & Relief	Inlay		$1200.
2594	2.85L	Glazed	Pewter	Plain light yellow color (also found in smaller sizes)	$125.
2599	1.0L	Etched	Inlay	Man shooting rifle at target, signed Quidenus (same scene as 2482)	$1100.
2607	1.5L	Cameo	Inlay	Three panels (master to 2608)	$700.
2607	2.15L	Cameo	Inlay		$800.
2607	1.5L	Relief	Inlay		$300.
2607	2.15L	Relief	Inlay		$350.
2608	.3L	Cameo	Inlay	Three panels: drinking, courting, and music (master is 2607)	$425.

2608 .3L, 2627 .5L, 2628 .5L

Number	Size	Type	Lid	Description	Value
2627	.3L	Cameo	Inlay	People with bicycles, signed Stahl, (master is 2686)	$600.
2627	.5L	Cameo	Inlay		$900.
2628	.5L	Cameo	Inlay	Three panels, bowling and tavern scenes, signed Stahl, ball on inlay (master is 2688)	$850.

2632 .5L, 2635 .5L, 2639 .5L

Number	Size	Type	Lid	Description	Value
2631	2.5L	Cameo	Inlay	Boar hunt stein, by Stahl (master to 2530)	$1800.
2632	.5L	Etched	Inlay	Bowling and tavern scene	$500.
2634	2.55L	Cameo	Inlay	Rodenstein stein, three panels, knights drinking, by Stahl, conical lid (master to 2652)	$1600.
2635	.5L	Etched	Inlay	Girl holding safety bicycle	$800.
2638	.5L	Etched	Inlay	Young girl	$600.
2639	.5L	Etched	Inlay	Blacksmith and cavalier stein, arms interlocked	$700.
2639	1.0L	Etched	Inlay		$900.
2640	.5L	Etched	Inlay	Barmaid and drinker, signed Quidenus	$550.

2638 .5L pewter lid: value $525., 2662 .5L, 2652 .5L

Number	Size	Type	Lid	Description	Value
2652	.25L	Cameo	Inlay	Rodenstein stein, three panels signed Stahl, conical lid (master is 2634)	$550.
2652	.5L	Cameo	Inlay		$900.
2662	.5L	Etched	Inlay	Student having drunken delusions, mice running all around	$1500.
2681	.5L	Etched	Inlay	Barmaid carrying six steins	$550.
2682	1.4L	Etched	Inlay	Girl holding grapes, signed Quidenus	$800.

Number	Size	Type	Lid	Description	Value
2683	.5L	Glazed	Pewter	Shaped like apple, red glaze	$150.
2683/177	.5L	Glazed	Pewter	Shaped like apple, red glaze with floral design	$350.
2684	.5L	Glazed	Pewter	Shaped like apple, green glaze	$150.
2684/178	.5L	Glazed	Pewter	Shaped like apple, green glaze with floral design	$350.
2685	.5L	Glazed	Pewter	Blue/green glaze	$125.
2685/179	.5L	Glazed	Pewter	Blue/green glaze with a floral design	$275.

2634 2.55L, 2686 2.5L, 2688 2.5L

Number	Size	Type	Lid	Description	Value
2686	2.5L	Cameo	Inlay	Bicycle scene, signed Stahl (master to 2627)	$1800.
2688	2.5L	Cameo	Inlay	Three panels, bowling and tavern scenes, ball on inlay, signed Stahl (master to 2628)	$1600.
2690	1.4L	Etched	Inlay	Men drinking and singing, jeweled base, signed Quidenus	$1250.
2691	2.75L	Etched	Inlay	Man with guitar in cellar	$1400.

2683/177 .5L, 2684/178 .5L, 2685/179 .5L

Number	Size	Type	Lid	Description	Value
2692	3.0L	Etched	Inlay	Tavern scene, barmaid and drinker (master to 2693)	$1400.
2693	.5L	Etched	Inlay	Tavern scene, barmaid and drinker (master is 2692)	$675.

2691 2.75L pewter lid: value $1150., 2692 3.0L

Number	Size	Type	Lid	Description	Value
2701/180	.5L	Glazed	Pewter	Shaped like apple, brown glaze	$350.
2702	4.8L	PUG	Pewter	Print under glaze blank body (see PUG Steins)	—
2714	.3L	Cameo	Inlay	Courting scenes (master is 2761)	$600.
2714	.5L	Cameo	Inlay		$800.
2715	.3L	Cameo	Inlay	Musical, dancing, and drinking scenes (master is 2757)	$600.
2715	.5L	Cameo	Inlay		$800.
2716	.5L	Etched	Inlay	Waitress serving dinner to two men, signed Quidenus	$650.
2716	1.0L	Etched	Inlay		$900.
2717	.5L	Etched & Glazed	Inlay	Venus target stein, nude in front of target	$2100.
2717	1.0L	Etched & Glazed	Inlay		$3200.
2718	.5L	Etched & Glazed	Inlay	David and Goliath stein, handle has holes for fingers	$2300.
2718	1.0L	Etched & Glazed	Inlay		$3400.

2716 1.0L, 2717 1.0L, 2718 1.0L

2715 .5L, 2756 .5L, 2772 .5L

Number	Size	Type	Lid	Description	Value
				Set of Twelve	
2719	.5L	Etched & Glazed	Inlay	Baker occupation	$1100.
2720	.5L	Etched & Glazed	Inlay	Tailor occupation	$1200.
2721	.5L	Etched & Glazed	Inlay	Cabinetmaker occupation	$1200.
2722	.5L	Etched & Glazed	Inlay	Shoemaker occupation	$1100.
2723	.5L	Etched & Glazed	Inaly	Carpenter occupation	$1300.
2724	.5L	Etched & Glazed	Inlay	Mason occupation	$1300.
2725	.5L	Etched & Glazed	Inlay	Artist (painter) occupation	$1500.
2726	.5L	Etched & Glazed	Inlay	Goldsmith occupation	$1400.
2727	.5L	Etched & Glazed	Inlay	Printer occupation	$1600.
2728	.5L	Etched & Glazed	Inlay	Brewer occupation	$1200.
2729	.5L	Etched & Glazed	Inlay	Blacksmith occupation	$1500.
2730	.5L	Etched & Glazed	Inlay	Butcher occupation	$1500.

2719 .5L, 2720 .5L, 2721 .5L

Occupation series

2722 .5L, 2723 .5L, 2724 .5L

2725 .5L, 2726 .5L, 2727 .5L

Occupation series

2728 .5L, 2729 .5L, 2730 .5L

Number	Size	Type	Lid	Description	Value
2745	.5L	Etched	Inlay	Man holding stein	$550.
2745	1.0L	Etched	Inlay		$800.
2751	2.5L	Etched	Inlay	Two men with tri-corner hats sitting at table smoking and drinking, signed Schlitt (master to 2752)	$1800.
2752	.5L	Etched	Inlay	Two men smoking and drinking, signed Schlitt (master is 2751)	$650.

Set of Four

Number	Size	Type	Lid	Description	Value
2753	.5L	Cameo	Inlay	Man, woman, and musicians in three panels	$800.
2754	.5L	Cameo	Inlay	Lovers, three panels	$850.
2755	.25L	Cameo	Inlay	Man and woman drinking, three panels	$575.
2755	.5L	Cameo	Inlay		$850.
2756	.3L	Cameo	Inlay	Lovers, three panels (master is 2762)	$575.
2756	.5L	Cameo	Inlay		$850.

2745 1.0L, 2765 1.0L, 2767 1.0L

2757 2.3L, 2761 2.3L, 2762 2.15L

Number	Size	Type	Lid	Description	Value
2757	2.3L	Cameo	Inlay	Musical, dancing, and drinking scenes (master to 2715)	$1600.
2761	2.3L	Cameo	Inlay	Courting scenes (master to 2714)	$1600.
2762	2.15L	Cameo	Inlay	Lovers, three panels (master to 2756)	$1600.
2764	5.8L	Etched	Inlay	Knight on white horse stein, turret lid, signed Schlitt (master to 2765)	$7000.
2765	.5L	Etched	Inlay	Knight on white horse stein, turret lid, signed Schlitt (master is 2764)	$2600.
2765	1.0L	Etched	Inlay		$3500.
2766	.5L	Etched	Inlay	Man drinking	$600.
2767	.5L	Etched	Inlay	Munich Child (matches plaque 1044/1014, stein 1014[2262], beaker 1014[2368])	$850.
2767	1.0L	Etched	Inlay		$1300.
2768	.5L	Etched	Inlay	People in Tyrolean clothes	$700.
2772	.5L	Relief	Pewter	Brown University	$150.

2693 .5L   2768 .5L   2766 .5L

2776 .5L, 2778 .5L, 2780 .5L

Number	Size	Type	Lid	Description	Value
2773	2.3L	Cameo	Inlay	Lovers	$1600.
2776	.5L	Etched	Inlay	Keeper of wine cellar	$800.
2777	3.1L	Etched	Inlay	Carnival stein, carnival player and drinkers, signed Schlitt (master to 2778)	$3000.
2778	.25L	Etched	Inlay	Carnival stein, carnival player and drinkers, signed Schlitt (master is 2777)	$750.
2778	.5L	Etched	Inlay		$1400.
2778	1.0L	Etched	Inlay		$1900.
2780	.5L	Etched	Inlay	Man playing guitar for lady	$675.
2780	1.0L	Etched	Inlay		$900.

2796 3.0L   2797 4.1L   2764 5.8L

Number	Size	Type	Lid	Description	Value
2782/6127	4.5L	Rookwood	Pewter	Man drinking	$650.
2782/6148	4.5L	Rookwood	Pewter	Woman	$800.
2783/6128	4.8L	Rookwood	Pewter	Man drinking	$700.
2783/6139	4.8L	Rookwood	Pewter	Man	$700.
2784/6129	2.2L	Rookwood	Pewter	Guitar player	$550.
2784/6140	2.2L	Rookwood	Pewter	Man with soft hat	$550.
2785/6130	2.2L	Rookwood	Pewter	Bagpipe player	$550.
2786/6131	2.2L	Rookwood	Pewter	Boy with flute	$550.
2787/6132	2.2L	Rookwood	Pewter	Man smoking	$550.
2787/6141	2.2L	Rookwood	Pewter	Man drinking	$550.
2788/6133	.5L	Rookwood	Pewter	Cavalier	$400.

2788/6133 .5L, 2788/6142 .5L, 2789/6145 .5L

Number	Size	Type	Lid	Description	Value
2788/6142	.5L	Rookwood	Pewter	Cavalier with pipe and stein (matches beaker 6142[2327])	$400.
2788/6143	.5L	Rookwood	Pewter	Man drinking	$400.
2788/6149	.5L	Rookwood	Pewter	Woman	$550.
2789/6134	.5L	Rookwood	Pewter	Man with pipe	$400.
2789/6144	.5L	Rookwood	Pewter	Drummer boy	$425.
2789/6145	.5L	Rookwood	Pewter	Man smoking pipe and drinking	$400.
2790/6135	.5L	Rookwood	Pewter	Man drinking	$400.
2790/6146	.5L	Rookwood	Pewter	Man drinking (matches beaker 6146[2327])	$400.

2790/6135 .5L, 2790/6146 .5L, 2790/6147 .5L

Number	Size	Type	Lid	Description	Value
2790/6147	.5L	Rookwood	Pewter	Bearded man	$400.
2791/6136	.5L	Rookwood	Pewter	Man drinking	$400.
2792/6137	.25L	Rookwood	Pewter	Cavalier with pipe and stein (matches beaker 6137[2327])	$350.
2793/6138	.25L	Rookwood	Pewter	Man smoking cigar	$350.

2792/6137 .25L, 2793/6138 .25L

2789/6134 .5L

2785/6130 2.2L, 2786/6131 2.2L, 2787/6132 2.2L

Number	Size	Type	Lid	Description	Value
2796	3.0L	Etched	Inlay	Scene of Heidelberg	$1800.
2797	4.1L	Etched	Inlay	Portrait of Richard Wagner (master to 2798)	$2300.
2798	.5L	Etched	Inlay	Portrait of Richard Wagner (master is 2797)	$700.
2799	2.1L	Etched	Inlay	Art nouveau design (master to 2800)	$475.
2800	.25L	Etched	Inlay	Art nouveau design (master is 2799)	$275.
2800	.5L	Etched	Inlay		$325.
2801	2.15L	Etched	Inlay	Art nouveau design (master to 2802)	$475.
2802	.25L	Etched	Inlay	Art nouveau design (master is 2801)	$250.
2802	.5L	Etched	Inlay		$300.
2807	.5L	Etched	Inlay	Tavern scene	$600.

Number	Size	Type	Lid	Description	Value
2808	.5L	Etched	Inlay	Girl bowling	$500.
2809	.5L	Etched	Inlay	Faithful Eckart, from the Goethe poem, signed Quidenus (sometimes found with *Rip Van Winkle* around base)	$700.
2810	2.15L	Etched	Inlay	Art nouveau design (master to 2811)	$475.
2811	.5L	Etched	Inlay	Art nouveau design (master is 2810)	$325.
2812	2.6L	Etched	Inlay	St. Hubert stein, art nouveau designs with skulls (master to 2813, matches bowl 2014)	$900.
2813	.5L	Etched	Inlay	St. Hubert stein, art nouveau designs with skulls (master is 2812, matches bowl 2014)	$450.
2823	.5L	Tapestry	Pewter	Girl with rifle	$325.
2823	1.0L	Tapestry	Pewter		$400.
2824	3.8L	Etched & Relief	Inlay	Town of Wartburg, houses and towers on lid, full color relief (master to 2828, mate to 2038)	$5000.
2825	3.5L	Etched	Inlay	Knight, troubadour, and jester, signed Schlitt	$4000.

2798 .5L, 2800 .5L, 2807 .5L

2809 .5L, 2813 .5L, 2878 .5L

2824 3.8L, 2825 3.5L

Number	Size	Type	Lid	Description	Value
2828	.5L	Etched & Relief	Inlay	Town of Wartburg, houses and towers on lid, full color relief (mate to 2829, master is 2824)	$2000.
2828	1.0L	Etched & Relief	Inlay		$2900.
2829	.5L	Etched & Relief	Inlay	Town of Rodenstein, houses and towers on lid, full color relief, frequently incorrectly called *Black Forest* stein (mate to 2828, master is 2038)	$1800.
2829	1.0L	Etched & Relief	Inlay		$2600.

2823 1.0L   2829 1.0L, 2828 1.0L

Number	Size	Type	Lid	Description	Value
2830	.5L	Etched	Inlay	Tyrolean girl	$450.
2831	.5L	Etched	Inlay	Owl on front, made for Siedel Science of Philadelphia Penn., founded 1895	$1150.
2832	.5L	Etched	Inlay	Woman in window	$425.

2845 .5L, 2831 .5L, 2832 .5L

Number	Size	Type	Lid	Description	Value
				Set of Six	
2833A	.3L	Etched	Inlay	Man in red cape and brown hat, with cane	$325.
2833A	.5L	Etched	Inlay		$425.
2833B	.3L	Etched	Inlay	Hunters in forest	$325.
2833B	.5L	Etched	Inlay		$425.
2833C	.3L	Etched	Inlay	Loreley River scene	$325.
2833C	.5L	Etched	Inlay		$425.
2833D	.3L	Etched	Inlay	Young man and young girl holding hands	$325.
2833D	.5L	Etched	Inlay		$425.
2833E	.3L	Etched	Inlay	Soldiers in forest in winter	$325.
2833E	.5L	Etched	Inlay		$425.
2833F	.3L	Etched	Inlay	Students drinking, signed M.C., steins in this series all have bases resembling bricks, thus the series is called the *Brick series*	$325.
2833F	.5L	Etched	Inlay		$425.
2835	2.65L	Cameo	Inlay	Three panels, woman in each panel (master to 2836)	$1400.
2836	.25L	Cameo	Inlay	Three panels, woman in each panel (master is 2835)	$475.
2836	.5L	Cameo	Inlay		$675.

Number	Size	Type	Lid	Description	Value
2844	.5L	Etched	Inlay	Three panels: farming, fishing, and hunting	$1000.
2845	.5L	Etched	Inlay	Tyrolean hunter	$600.

2833A .5L, 2833B .5L, 2833C .5L

Brick series

2833D .5L, 2833E .5L, 2833F .5L

Number	Size	Type	Lid	Description	Value
2869	2.9L	Etched & Relief	Inlay	Munich Child and scenes of Munich, full color relief lion and shield on inlay, signed Hein (master to 2917)	$4000.
2869	2.9L	Etched & Relief	Inlay	Same body as above, but with a *Hofbrauhaus* on the inlay	$5800.
2871	1.0L	Etched	Inlay	Cornell University stein, buildings and song	$1100.
2872	.5L	Etched	Inlay	Cornell University stein, three scenes of buildings, Cornell University steins are usually marked "Made Exclusively For Rothschild Bros."	$800.

2869 2.9L, 2869 *Hofbrauhaus* 2.9L   2835 2.65L

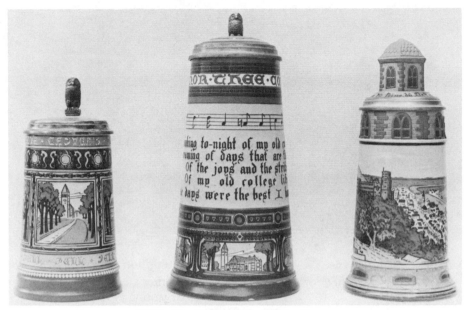

2872 .5L, 2871 1.0L, 2894 .5L

Number	Size	Type	Lid	Description	Value
2878	.5L	Tapestry	Pewter	Tyrolean girls	$325.
2878	1.0L	Tapestry	Pewter		$400.
2880	.5L	Etched	Inlay	Tavern scene	$425.
2880	1.0L	Etched	Inlay		$550.

Set of Four

Number	Size	Type	Lid	Description	Value
2886	.5L	Etched	Inlay	*The notables,* five politicians seated at table	$500.
2886	1.0L	Etched	Inlay		$650.
2887	.5L	Etched	Inlay	Knights drinking	$500.
2888	.5L	Etched	Inlay	Three men walking down road	$500.
2888	1.0L	Etched	Inlay		$650.
2889	.5L	Etched	Inlay	Man on horse, holding stein	$500.
2891	.5L	Etched	Inlay	Art nouveau design	$250.
2892	.5L	Etched	Inlay	Art nouveau design	$275.
2893	3.25L	PUG	Pewter	Print under glaze blank body (see PUG Steins), also smaller sizes	—
2894	.5L	Etched	Inlay	Heidelberg student stein, view of Heidelberg, Perkeo, and Rodenstein on rear of stein, turret roof on inlay	$2000.

2886 .5L, 2888 .5L, 2887 .5L

Number	Size	Type	Lid	Description	Value
2900	.5L	Etched	Inlay	Argentina Quilmes stein, brewery in Argentina, 1904 version	$450.
2900	.5L	Etched	Inlay	1906 version	$450.
2900	.5L	Etched	Inlay	1931 version, bottom marked: *Mettlach, Saar Basin*	$400.
2903	.5L	Etched	Inlay	Art nouveau design	$300.

2900 "1904" .5L, 2900 "1906" .5L, 2900 "1931" .5L

Number	Size	Type	Lid	Description	Value
2911	2.0L	Etched	Inlay	Art nouveau design	$400.
2911	3.2L	Etched	Inlay		$475.
2912	2.0L	Etched	Inlay	Art nouveau design	$400.
2912	3.0L	Etched	Inlay		$475.
2917	.5L	Etched & Relief	Inlay	Munich Child and scenes of Munich, full color relief, lion and shield on inlay, signed Hein (master is 2869)	$2200.
2917	1.0L	Etched & Relief	Inlay		$3200.

2922 1.0L, 2936 .5L

Number	Size	Type	Lid	Description	Value
2921	2.8L	Etched	Inlay	Hunter drinking in front of campfire (master to 2922)	$900.
2922	.25L	Etched	Inlay	Hunter drinking in front of campfire (master is 2921)	$300.
2922	.5L	Etched	Inlay		$450.
2922	1.0L	Etched	Inlay		$550.
2930	3.6L	Relief	Inlay	Man and woman and verse (master to 2931)	$375.
2931	.5L	Relief	Inlay	Man and woman and verse (master is 2930)	$180.
2934	.3L	Etched	Inlay	Art nouveau design	$275.
2934	.5L	Etched	Inlay		$325.

Number	Size	Type	Lid	Description	Value
2935	.3L	Etched	Inlay	Art nouveau design	$275.
2935	.5L	Etched	Inlay		$325.
2936	.5L	Etched	Inlay	Elk's Club stein	$350.
			Set of Three		
2937	.5L	Etched	Inlay	Nightwatchman	$575.
2937	1.0L	Etched	Inlay		$700.
2938	.5L	Etched	Inlay	Hunter with his dog	$575.
2938	1.0L	Etched	Inlay		$700.
2939	.5L	Etched	Inlay	Waitress	$575.
2939	1.0L	Etched	Inlay		$700.

2937 1.0L, 2938 1.0L, 2939 1.0L

Number	Size	Type	Lid	Description	Value
2942	.5L	Relief	Inlay	Simple design and verse	$150.
2943	.5L	Relief	Inlay	Two people and verse	$160.
2944	.5L	Relief	Inlay	Simple design	$140.
2945	.5L	Relief	Inlay	Simple design	$150.
			Set of Three		
2949	.5L	Cameo	Pewter	Munich Child and coat of arms	$475.
2949	1.0L	Cameo	Pewter		$800.
2950	.5L	Cameo	Pewter	Bavarian coat of arms	$475.
2950	1.0L	Cameo	Pewter		$800.
2951	.5L	Cameo	Pewter	Prussian eagle	$475.
2951	1.0L	Cameo	Pewter		$800.

2949 1.0L, 2950 1.0L, 2951 1.0L

Number	Size	Type	Lid	Description	Value
2956	3.1L	Etched	Inlay	Bowling scene (master to 2957)	$800.
2957	.5L	Etched	Inlay	Bowling scene (master is 2956)	$450.
2958	2.8L	Etched	Inlay	Boy bowling (master to 2959)	$750.
2959	.5L	Etched	Inlay	Boy bowling (master is 2958)	$450.
2959	1.0L	Etched	Inlay		$550.
2966	.5L	Tapestry	Pewter	Man drinking	$300.
2966	1.0L	Tapestry	Pewter		$375.

2957 .5L, 2959 .5L, 2966 1.0L

Number	Size	Type	Lid	Description	Value
2967	.5L	Tapestry	Pewter	Farmers with piglets	$325.
2967	1.0L	Tapestry	Pewter		$400.
2993	2.0L	Etched	Inlay	Art Nouveau design (master to 2994)	$475.
2993	3.3L	Etched	Inlay		$550.
2994	.25L	Etched	Inlay	Art nouveau design (master is 2993)	$300.
2994	.5L	Etched	Inlay		$350.
3000	.5L	Etched	Pewter	Three panels with women	$300.
3000	1.0L	Etched	Pewter		$400.
3001	.5L	Etched	Pewter	Man walking	$300.
3002	.5L	Etched	Pewter	People walking	$350.
3003	.5L	Etched	Pewter	Man in short coat	$300.
3004	.5L	Etched	Pewter	Man with drink	$300.
3004	1.0L	Etched	Pewter		$400.
3005	.5L	Etched	Pewter	Man with drink	$300.
3005	1.0L	Etched	Pewter		$400.
3008	3.35L	Glazed	Pewter	Plain pitcher (also smaller sizes)	$125.
3024	1.8L	Relief	Inlay	Cavalier	$250.
3024	3.6L	Relief	Inlay		$300.
3025	3.0L	Relief	Inlay	Bowling scene	$300.

3000 .5L, 3002 .5L, 3003 .5L

3034 .5L, 3080/534 .5L, 3078/419 .5L

Number	Size	Type	Lid	Description	Value
3034	.5L	Cameo	Inlay	Mrs. Von Schiller	$600.
3034	1.0L	Cameo	Inlay		$750.
3042	4.1L	Etched	Pewter	Man and woman drinking	$500.
3043	.5L	Etched & Glazed	Inlay	Munich stein, shield of Munich (mate to 2024)	$1600.
3078	1.0L	Bavaria	Pewter	*Prosit*	$150.
3078/419	.5L	Bavaria	Inlay	Owl	$200.
3078/437	.5L	Bavaria	Inlay	Man and woman, marked Bavaria under castle mark, this style is usually found on grey body, scenes are hand painted	$150.
3080/439	.5L	Bavaria	Inlay	Man and woman dancing	$150.
3080/534	.5L	Bavaria	Inlay	Black child with mug	$275.
3084	3.1L	Tapestry	Pewter	Postman (master to 3085)	$600.
3085	.25L	Tapestry	Pewter	Postman (master is 3084)	$250.
3085	.5L	Tapestry	Pewter		$325.
3085	1.0L	Tapestry	Pewter		$400.
3086	3.1L	Tapestry	Pewter	Tyrolean girl (master to 3087)	$600.
3087	.25L	Tapestry	Pewter	Tyrolean girl (master is 3086)	$250.
3087	.5L	Tapestry	Pewter		$325.
3087	1.0L	Tapestry	Pewter		$400.

Number	Size	Type	Lid	Description	Value
				Set of Five	
3089	.5L	Etched	Inlay	*Diogenes* stein, Diogenes sitting in barrel, signed Schlitt (master is 3099)	$950.
3089	1.0L	Etched	Inlay		$1400.
3090	.5L	Etched	Inlay	Two girls and troubadour, signed Schlitt	$800.
3090	1.0L	Etched	Inlay		$1000.
3091	.5L	Etched	Inlay	Drinking knight stein, signed Schlitt	$1000.
3091	1.0L	Etched	Inlay		$1400.
3092	.5L	Etched	Inlay	Whiskey man stein, holding a glass, signed Schlitt	$850.
3092	1.0L	Etched	Inlay		$1200.
3093	.5L	Etched	Inlay	Troll stein, signed Schlitt	$1400.

3089 .5L, 3090 .5L, 3091 .5L

Number	Size	Type	Lid	Description	Value
3094/421	3.8L	Bavaria	Pewter	Floral design	$175.
3094/514	2.9L	Bavaria	Pewter	Flowers in basket	$200.
3099	3.0L	Etched	Inlay	Diogenes stein, Diogenes sitting in barrel, signed Schlitt (master to 3089)	$2700.
3119	1.0L	Etched	Inlay	Prussian eagle, golden tan background	$2400.

Number	Size	Type	Lid	Description	Value
3135	.5L	Etched	Inlay	American flag stein, flags and eagle (sometimes has F.O.E. painted on stein)	$1250.

Set of Three

Number	Size	Type	Lid	Description	Value
3142	.5L	Etched	Inlay	Bavarian scene	$600.
3142	1.0L	Etched	Inlay		$850.
3143	.5L	Etched	Inlay	Tyrolean scene	$600.
3143	1.0L	Etched	Inlay		$850.
3144	.5L	Etched	Inlay	Black Forest scene	$600.
3144	1.0L	Etched	Inlay		$850.

3092 .5L, 3093 .5L, 3085 1.0L

Number	Size	Type	Lid	Description	Value
3156	.5L	Etched	Inlay	Chicago stein, three buildings, gold dome on lid	$2800.
3167	.5L	Etched	Inlay	Waitresses and waiters with steins, signed Hohlwein	$375.
3168	.5L	Etched	Inlay	Hunter on horse with hound, signed Hohlwein	$375.
3169	.5L	Etched	Inlay	Deer, signed Hohlwein	$350.
3170	.5L	Etched	Inlay	Men walking on winter night, signed Hohlwein	$350.
3171	.5L	Etched	Inlay	Hunter and deer, signed Hohlwein	$375.
3172	.5L	Etched	Inlay	Fat man singing, signed Hohlwein	$375.

3142 1.0L, 3143 1.0L, 3144 1.0L

Number	Size	Type	Lid	Description	Value
3173	.5L	Etched	Inlay	Man and woman, signed Hohlwein	$375.
3177	2.2L	Cameo	Inlay	Hunting scenes	$1500.

3170 .5L, 3171 .5L, 3172 .5L

Number	Size	Type	Lid	Description	Value
3185	.5L	PUG	Inlay	Print under glaze blank body (see PUG Steins)	—
				Set of Three	
3189	.5L	Etched	Inlay	Unusual shape, blue glaze body with small medallion surrounded by rope design, woman with turkey on tray, signed Ringer	$450.
3191	.5L	Etched	Inlay	Yellow glaze body, man with beer glass, signed Ringer	$450.
3193	.5L	Etched	Inlay	Red glaze body, man with jug, signed Ringer	$450.

3135 .5L, 3156 .5L   3202 .5L

Number	Size	Type	Lid	Description	Value
3200	.5L	Etched	Inlay	Scene of Heidelberg	$650.
3202	.5L	Etched	Inlay	Car stein, automobile with driver and passenger	$1500.
3219	.5L	Etched	Inlay	Men drinking	$600.
3220	.5L	Etched	Inlay	Couple dancing, signed Quidenus	$600.
3221	.5L	Etched	Inlay	Old man and young man toasting, signed Quidenus	$650.

Number	Size	Type	Lid	Description	Value
				Set of Six	
3249	.5L	Etched	Inlay	Two men drinking	$450.
3250	.5L	Etched	Inlay	People dining	$450.
3251	.5L	Etched	Inlay	Hunter and young girl	$450.
3252	.5L	Etched	Inlay	Couple drinking	$450.
3253	.5L	Etched	Inlay	Card players	$450.
3254	.5L	Etched	Inlay	People eating and drinking	$450.

3219 .5L, 3220 .5L, 3221 .5L

Number	Size	Type	Lid	Description	Value
3257	2.0L	PUG	Pewter	Print under glaze blank body (see PUG Steins)	—
3279	.5L	Etched	Inlay	*Prosit* on front of stein, boy with sword, sausage, and chicken, walking away from farm girl, signed Hohlwein	$400.
3281	.5L	Etched	Inlay	*Hoch Sport* on front of stein, jockey and tennis player, signed Hohlwein	$400.
3329	.5L	Etched & Relief	Inlay	Five cavaliers gambling at cards, lady luck and devil in rear of stein in full color relief, signed Quidenus	$1000.
3329	1.0L	Etched & Relief	Inlay		$1300.

3200 .5L

3250 .5L, 3253 .5L

3342/546 .4L

3329 .5L

3333 3.0L

Number	Size	Type	Lid	Description	Value
3332	3.0L	Etched	Inlay	Scene of Nurnberg	$2000.
3333	3.0L	Etched	Inlay	Scene of Rheinstein	$2000.
3342	.4L	Bavaria	Inlay	Four sides, geometric design	$100.
3342/546	.4L	Bavaria	Inlay	Four sides, suits of cards	$325.
3343	.4L	Bavaria	Inlay	Six sides, floral design	$125.
3343/547	.4L	Bavaria	Inlay	Six sides, six people	$200.
3343/548	.4L	Bavaria	Inlay	Six sides, skiing scenes	$250.
3343/549	.4L	Bavaria	Inlay	Six sides, mountain climber	$250.
3344/551	.5L	Bavaria	Inlay	Six sides, students drinking	$250.
3344/552	.5L	Bavaria	Inlay	Six sides, two student duelers	$250.

5000 series steins, in the 1.0L size, originally had pewter rims on the base. If found without this rim, they are worth about 30% less.

5001	4.6L	Faience	Pewter	Coat of arms	$950.
5002	4.6L	Faience	Pewter	Three scenes with people	$950.
5003	5.0L	Faience	Pewter	Buildings	$950.
5004	.5L	Faience	Pewter	Coat of arms	$375.
5005	.5L	Faience	Pewter	Figure of man	$425.

5006 Munich .5L, 5013 Munich .5L, 5019 1.0L

5015 1.35L, 5016 1.35L, 5020 3.1L

Number	Size	Type	Lid	Description	Value
5006	.5L	Faience	Pewter	Building	$400.
5006	.5L	Faience	Pewter	Munich scene	$400.
5013	.5L	Faience	Pewter	Munich scene	$500.
5013	1.0L	Faience	Pewter		$1000.
5013/965	.5L	Faience	Pewter	Emblem with many colors	$400.
5014	.25L	Faience	Pewter	Flowers	$325.
5015	1.35L	Faience	Pewter	Bird	$900.
5016	1.35L	Faience	Pewter	Angels	$800.
5018	2.6L	Faience	Pewter	Floral design	$750.
5019	.5L	Faience	Pewter	Floral design	$400.
5019	1.0L	Faience	Pewter		$950.
5020	3.1L	Faience	Pewter	Munich Child	$850.
5021	5.0L	Faience	Pewter	Rothenburg scene	$900.
5022	.5L	Faience	Pewter	Rural scene	$450.
5022	1.0L	Faience	Pewter		$1000.
5023	1.0L	Faience	Pewter	Prussian eagle	$1500.
5024	1.0L	Faience	Pewter	Floral, very fancy pewter	$1300.
5028	1.0L	Faience	Pewter	Cupid on horseback	$1400.

5013/965 .5L, 5190 .5L, 5191

Number	Size	Type	Lid	Description	Value
5030	1.0L	Faience	Pewter	Bayreuth scene	$1000.
5034	1.15L	Faience	None	Bayreuth scene	$600.
5188	.5L	Faience	Pewter	Man drinking	$400.
5189	.5L	Faience	Pewter	Man	$350.

5022 1.0L, 5023 1.0L, 5024 1.0L

Number	Size	Type	Lid	Description	Value
5190	.5L	Faience	Pewter	Man drinking	$400.
5191	.3L	Faience	Pewter	Man drinking	$300.
5192	5.0L	Faience	Pewter	Man drinking	$950.
5193	5.0L	Faience	Pewter	Man drinking	$950.
5393	1.0L	Faience	Pewter	Diana	$1400.
5394	1.0L	Faience	Pewter	Mercury and Pegasus	$1400.
5395	.5L	Faience	Pewter	Dancing couple	$550.
5442	1.0L	Faience	Pewter	Cavalier drinking and smoking	$1400.
5443	1.0L	Faience	Pewter	Man with beer stein	$1250.

5192 5.0L, 5193 5.0L

5028 1.0L, 5393 1.0L, 5394 1.0L

4. PUG Steins by Decoration Number

Print under glaze, or so-called PUG, decorations were transfer printed on several different blank stein forms. The printed decoration numbers on the bottom of these steins are listed below in numerical order, along with the body style that most frequently carries that decoration. As mentioned at the beginning of section 3, Rookwood steins (with incised mold numbers 2782 to 2793 and decoration numbers in the 6000's), and faience steins (with numbers in the 5000's) are not strictly considered to be PUG steins and are listed in the previous section.

It should be noted that Mettlach on occasion sold the blank steins without any PUG decoration. Some of these blanks were subsequently hand painted, but unlike the PUG's, these decorations can be felt or seen as raised. Price ranges for these variants can be found in Appendix A.

Number	Size	Lid	Description	Value
225(2184)	.3L	Inlay	Landscape	$170.
225(2184)	.5L	Inlay		$200.
225(2183)	3.25L	Inlay		$350.
		Set of Three		
238(1909)	.5L	Pewter	Tyrolean man (matches beaker 238[2327])	$200.
239(1909)	.5L	Pewter	Man and woman (matches beaker 239 [2327])	$200.
240(1909)	.5L	Pewter	Hunter (matches beaker 240[2327])	$200.

Number	Size	Lid	Description	Value
566(1526)	.5L	Pewter	Young hunter with dachshunds	$160.
567(1526)	.5L	Pewter	4F motif	$150.
568(1526)	.5L	Pewter	Musical symbols	$140.
569(1526)	.5L	Pewter	*Prosit*	$130.

Set of Three

Number	Size	Lid	Description	Value
580(1530)	.5L	Inlay	Hunter smoking	$275.
581(1530)	.5L	Inlay	Student smoking	$275.
582(1530)	.5L	Inlay	Man smoking	$275.
586(1526)	.5L	Pewter	Barmaid	$140.
587(1526)	.5L	Pewter	Man proposing toast	$150.
588(1526)	.5L	Pewter	Barmaid	$140.
589(1526)	.5L	Pewter	Tavern scene	$150.
590(1526)	.5L	Pewter	Tavern scene	$150.
591(1526)	.5L	Pewter	Lovers	$150.
592(1526)	.5L	Pewter	Tavern scene	$150.
595(1526)	1.0L	Pewter	Cavalier	$175.
596(1526)	1.0L	Pewter	Cavalier	$175.
597(1526)	1.0L	Pewter	Hunter	$175.
598(1526)	1.0L	Pewter	Marksman	$175.
599(1526)	1.0L	Pewter	Soldier	$175.
600(1526)	1.0L	Pewter	Soldier	$175.
601(1526)	.5L	Pewter	Goblin	$160.
602(1526)	.5L	Pewter	Drinkers	$160.

225(2184) .5L

626(280) .5L, 678(280) .5L

595(1526) 1.0L, 596(1526) 1.0L, 599(1526) 1.0L

Number	Size	Lid	Description	Value
603(1526)	.5L	Pewter	Drinkers	$160.
604(1526)	.5L	Pewter	Firemen symbols	$200.
606(1526)	.25L	Pewter	Clown	$120.
607(1526)	.25L	Pewter	Fiddler	$120.
608(1526)	.25L	Pewter	Man and woman	$120.
611(1526)	.25L	Pewter	People dining	$120.
612(1526)	.5L	Pewter	Munich Child	$175.
615(1526)	.25L	Pewter	Man with guitar	$120.
622(1855)	.5L	Pewter	Musicians	$150.
624(1526)	1.0L	Pewter	Lovers, signed CK	$175.
625(1526)	1.0L	Pewter	*Comfort of the languish*	$190.
626(280)	.5L	Pewter	Gnomes drinking	$190.
629(1526)	.25L	Pewter	Page with wine	$125.
631(1526)	.25L	Pewter	Munich Child	$150.
632(1526)	1.0L	Pewter	Munich Child	$225.
639(1908)	1.0L	Pewter	Woman with beer glass	$195.
642(1526)	.5L	Pewter	Lovers	$170.
644(1526)	3.0L	Pewter	Lady	$300.
660(1526)	.5L	Pewter	Man playing bagpipe	$160.
661(1526)	.5L	Pewter	Cavaliers	$160.

727(1909) .5L, 726(1909) .5L, 732(1909) .5L

Number	Size	Lid	Description	Value
662(1526)	.5L	Pewter	4F symbols	$175.
663(1526)	.5L	Pewter	Craftsman	$165.
664(1526)	.5L	Pewter	Woman and verse	$150.
665(1526)	.5L	Pewter	Man and beer barrel	$150.
673(1526)	.5L	Pewter	Gnomes	$175.
674(1526)	1.0L	Pewter	Old woman	$225.
676(1526)	1.0L	Pewter	Man and woman	$225.
677(1526)	.5L	Pewter	People talking	$175.
678(280)	.5L	Pewter	Carrying beer barrel	$250.
680(1526)	1.0L	Pewter	Student	$190.
682(1526)	.5L	Pewter	Drunken gnomes	$160.
702(1909)	.5L	Pewter	High-spirited parade	$275.
702(1526)	1.0L	Pewter		$300.
702(1526)	2.0L	Pewter		$350.
702(1526)	3.0L	Pewter		$375.
715(1909)	.5L	Pewter	Drunken revelers	$175.
726(1909)	.5L	Pewter	Steins with legs, filling up at tap	$275.
727(1909)	.3L	Pewter	Bowling gnomes, signed Schlitt	$180.
727(1909)	.5L	Pewter		$250.
732(1909)	.5L	Pewter	Owl shining lantern on drunken man, signed Schlitt	$275.

The military steins made by Mettlach have decoration numbers that are duplicative, inconsistent, and erratic. It thus makes the most sense to list these in order by units.

Number	Size	Lid	Description	Value
754(2140)	.5L	Pewter	*1. Garde-Regt. zu Fuss*	$465.
743(2140)	.5L	Pewter	*2. Garde-Regt. zu Fuss*	$465.
747(2140)	.5L	Pewter	*3. Garde-Regt. zu Fuss*	$465.
741(2140)	.5L	Pewter	*Garde-Grenadier-Regt. Nr. 1*	$465.
745(2140)	.5L	Pewter	*Garde-Grenadier-Regt. Nr. 2*	$465.
749(2140)	.5L	Pewter	*Garde-Grenadier-Regt. Nr. 3*	$465.
811(2140)	.5L	Pewter	*Grenadier-Regt. Nr. 2*	$465.
843(2140)	.5L	Pewter	*Grenadier-Regt. Nr. 4*	$465.
902(2140)	.5L	Pewter	*Grenadier-Regt. Nr. 7*	$465.
903(2140)	.5L	Pewter	*Grenadier-Regt. Nr. 10*	$465.
904(2140)	.5L	Pewter	*Grenadier-Regt. Nr. 11*	$465.
774(2140)	.5L	Pewter	*Grenadier-Regt. Nr. 12*	$465.
866(2140)	.5L	Pewter	*Infanterie-Regt. Nr. 18*	$450.
759(2140)	.5L	Pewter	*Infanterie-Regt. Nr. 20*	$450.
824(2140)	.5L	Pewter	*Infanterie-Regt. Nr. 21*	$450.
891(2140)	.5L	Pewter	*Infanterie-Regt. Nr. 22*	$450.
758(2140)	.5L	Pewter	*Infanterie-Regt. Nr. 24*	$450.

747(2140) .5L, 741(2140) .5L, 843(2140) .5L

Number	Size	Lid	Description	Value
767(2140)	.5L	Pewter	*Infanterie-Regt. Nr. 26*	$450.
920(2140)	.5L	Pewter	*Infanterie-Regt. Nr. 28*	$450.
(2140)	.5L	Pewter	*Infanterie-Regt. Nr. 32*	$450.
849(2140)	.5L	Pewter	*Infanterie-Regt. Nr. 33*	$450.
769(2140)	.5L	Pewter	*Infanterie-Regt. Nr. 36*	$450.
889(2140)	.5L	Pewter	*Infanterie-Regt. Nr. 38*	$450.
(2140)	.5L	Pewter	*Infanterie-Regt. Nr. 40*	$450.
847(2140)	.5L	Pewter	*Infanterie-Regt. Nr. 43*	$450.
839(2140)	.5L	Pewter	*Infanterie-Regt. Nr. 46*	$450.
761(2140)	.5L	Pewter	*Infanterie-Regt. Nr. 48*	$450.
895(2140)	.5L	Pewter	*Infanterie-Regt. Nr. 49*	$450.
760(2140)	.5L	Pewter	*Infanterie-Regt. Nr. 52*	$450.
813(2140)	.5L	Pewter	*Infanterie-Regt. Nr. 54*	$450.
905(2140)	.5L	Pewter	*Infanterie-Regt. Nr. 58*	$450.
893(2140)	.5L	Pewter	*Infanterie-Regt. Nr. 62*	$450.
756(2140)	.5L	Pewter	*Infanterie-Regt. Nr. 64*	$450.
922(2140)	.5L	Pewter	*Infanterie-Regt. Nr. 68*	$450.
771(2140)	.5L	Pewter	*Infanterie-Regt. Nr. 71*	$450.
773(2140)	.5L	Pewter	*Infanterie-Regt. Nr. 72*	$450.
872(2140)	.5L	Pewter	*Infanterie-Regt. Nr. 73*	$450.
873(2140)	.5L	Pewter	*Infanterie-Regt. Nr. 74*	$450.
875(2140)	.5L	Pewter	*Infanterie-Regt. Nr. 77*	$450.
876(2140)	.5L	Pewter	*Infanterie-Regt. Nr. 78*	$450.

767(2140) .5L, 849(2140) .5L, 761(2140) .5L

808(2140) .5L, 810(2140) .5L, 786(2140) .5L

Number	Size	Lid	Description	Value
877(2140)	.5L	Pewter	*Infanterie-Regt. Nr. 79*	$450.
(2140)	.5L	Pewter	*Infanterie-Regt. Nr. 82*	$450.
879(2140)	.5L	Pewter	*Infanterie-Regt. Nr. 91*	$450.
880(2140)	.5L	Pewter	*Infanterie-Regt. Nr. 92*	$450.
772(2140)	.5L	Pewter	*Infanterie-Regt. Nr. 93*	$450.
1056(2140)	.5L	Pewter	*Infanterie-Regt. Nr. 119*	$500.
867(2140)	.5L	Pewter	*Infanterie-Regt. Nr. 128*	$450.
(2140)	.5L	Pewter	*Infanterie-Regt. Nr. 140*	$450.
(2140)	.5L	Pewter	*Infanterie-Regt. Nr. 156*	$450.
(2140)	.5L	Pewter	*Infanterie-Regt. Nr. 158*	$450.
752(2140)	.5L	Pewter	*Garde-Jager-Bataillon*	$550.
750(2140)	.5L	Pewter	*Garde-Schutzen-Bataillon*	$550.
809(2140)	.5L	Pewter	*Jager-Bataillon Nr. 1*	$525.
810(2140)	.5L	Pewter	*Jager-Bataillon Nr. 2*	$525.
808(2140)	.5L	Pewter	*Jager-Bataillon Nr. 3*	$525.
810(2140)	.5L	Pewter	*Jager-Bataillon Nr. 4*	$525.
912(2140)	.5L	Pewter	*Jager-Bataillon Nr. 5*	$525.

Number	Size	Lid	Description	Value
810(2140)	.5L	Pewter	*Jager-Bataillon Nr. 7*	$525.
808(2140)	.5L	Pewter	*Jager-Bataillon Nr. 9*	$525.
809(2140)	.5L	Pewter	*Jager-Bataillon Nr. 11*	$525.
790(2140)	.5L	Pewter	*1. Garde-Feld-Artillerie-Regt.*	$475.
787(2140)	.5L	Pewter	*2. Garde-Feld-Artillerie-Regt.*	$475.
790(2140)	.5L	Pewter	*2. berittene Batterie des 2. Garde-Feld-Artillerie-Regt.*	$475.
765(2140)	.5L	Pewter	*Feld-Artillerie-Regt. Nr. 3*	$450.
792(2140)	.5L	Pewter	*Feld-Artillerie-Regt. Nr. 4*	$450.
881(2140)	.5L	Pewter	*Feld-Artillerie-Regt. Nr. 10*	$450.
818(2140)	.5L	Pewter	*Feld-Artillerie-Regt. Nr. 17*	$450.
794(2140)	.5L	Pewter	*Feld-Artillerie-Regt. Nr. 18*	$450.
(2140)	.5L	Pewter	*Feld-Artillerie-Regt. Nr. 20*	$450.
907(2140)	.5L	Pewter	*Feld-Artillerie-Regt. Nr. 21*	$450.
882(2140)	.5L	Pewter	*Feld-Artillerie-Regt. Nr. 26*	$450.
740(2140)	.5L	Pewter	*Garde-Pionnier-Bataillon*	$525.
799(2140)	.5L	Pewter	*Pionnier-Bataillon Nr. 4*	$500.
894(2140)	.5L	Pewter	*Pionnier-Bataillon Nr. 10*	$500.
786(2140)	.5L	Pewter	*Eisenbahn-Regt. Nr. 1*	$525.
786(2140)	.5L	Pewter	*Eisenbahn-Regt. Nr. 3*	$525.
801(2140)	.5L	Pewter	*Garde-Train-Bataillon*	$525.
796(2140)	.5L	Pewter	*Train-Bataillon Nr. 3*	$500.
836(2140)	.5L	Pewter	*Train-Bataillon Nr. 5*	$500.
789(2140)	.5L	Pewter	*Garde-du-Corps*	$600.
(2140)	.5L	Pewter	*1. Garde-Dragoner-Regt.*	$600.
782(2140)	.5L	Pewter	*2. Garde-Dragoner-Regt.*	$600.

Number	Size	Lid	Description	Value
753(2140)	.5L	Pewter	*Leibgarde-Husaren-Regt.*	$575.
783(2140)	.5L	Pewter	*1. Garde-Ulanen-Regt.*	$550.
784(2140)	.5L	Pewter	*2. Garde-Ulanen-Regt.*	$550.
742(2140)	.5L	Pewter	*3. Garde-Ulanen-Regt.*	$550.
1071(2140)	.5L	Pewter	*Kurassier-Regt. Nr. 4*	$575.
776(2140)	.5L	Pewter	*Kurassier-Regt. Nr. 6*	$575.
776(2140)	.5L	Pewter	*Kurassier-Regt. Nr. 7*	$575.
777(2140)	.5L	Pewter	*Dragoner-Regt. Nr. 2*	$550.
815(2140)	.5L	Pewter	*Dragoner-Regt. Nr. 3*	$550.
808(2140)	.5L	Pewter	*Dragoner-Regt. Nr. 8*	$550.
886(2140)	.5L	Pewter	*Dragoner-Regt. Nr. 19*	$550.
822(2140)	.5L	Pewter	*Husaren-Regt. Nr. 1*	$550.
831(2140)	.5L	Pewter	*Husaren-Regt. Nr. 2*	$550.
746(2140)	.5L	Pewter	*Husaren-Regt. Nr. 3*	$550.
911(2140)	.5L	Pewter	*Husaren-Regt. Nr. 6*	$550.
735(2140)	.5L	Pewter	*Husaren-Regt. Nr. 7*	$550.
807(2140)	.5L	Pewter	*Husaren-Regt. Nr. 10*	$550.
(2140)	.5L	Pewter	*Husaren-Regt. Nr. 13*	$550.
884(2140)	.5L	Pewter	*Husaren-Regt. Nr. 17*	$550.
899(2140)	.5L	Pewter	*Ulanen-Regt. Nr. 2*	$550.
(2140)	.5L	Pewter	*Ulanen-Regt. Nr. 3*	$550.
828(2140)	.5L	Pewter	*Ulanen-Regt. Nr. 6*	$550.
817(2140)	.5L	Pewter	*Ulanen-Regt. Nr. 9*	$550.

742(2140) .5L, 886(2140) .5L, 883(2140) .5L

Number	Size	Lid	Description	Value
853(2140)	.5L	Pewter	*Ulanen-Regt. Nr. 12*	$575.
883(2140)	.5L	Pewter	*Ulanen-Regt. Nr. 13*	$550.
893(2140)	.5L	Pewter	*Unteroffiziersschule Ettlingen*	$600.
(2140)	.5L	Pewter	*S.W. Africa Schutztruppen*	$1200.
(2140)	.5L	Pewter	*Luftschiffer 1894-1896*	$1800.

900(2227) 4.35L

(2140) *S.W. Africa Schutztruppen* .5L

The order now returns to the decoration numbers.

Number	Size	Lid	Description	Value
900(2227)	4.35L	Inlay	Military scenes, lid has large eagle mounted on it, with spread wings	$2500.
941(2140)	.5L	Pewter	Tavern, beer barometer	$260.
941(1526)	3.0L	Pewter		$375.
942(2140)	.5L	Pewter	Nightwatchman and rooster	$250.
942(1909)	.5L	Pewter		$165.
943(1909)	.5L	Pewter	Knight breaking open beer barrel	$280.
943(1526)	1.0L	Pewter		$300.
949(1909)	.5L	Pewter	Fancy gentleman	$170.
952(2140)	.5L	Pewter	Bicycle rider	$300.

956(2178) 2.5L, 953(2183) 3.25L

957(2181) .25L, 958(2181) .25L, 959(2177) .25L, 962(2179) .25L

Number	Size	Lid	Description	Value
953(2183)	3.25L	Inlay	Gnomes drinking, by Schlitt (master to 966 and 967[2184], beakers 1032 and 1033[2368] matches coaster set 1032)	$400.
954(2176)	2.7L	Pewter	Knight drinking, signed Schlitt (master to 959 and 960[2177])	$600.
955(2271)	.5L	Pewter	Tavern scene, signed Schlitt, (matches bowl 2226/1062, master to 958[2181] and 957[2181])	$275.
955(2180)	3.3L	Pewter		$650.
956(2178)	2.5L	Pewter	Gnomes feasting, signed Schlitt (master to 961 and 962[2179])	$500.
957(2181)	.25L	Pewter	Barmaid, by Schlitt (master is 955[2180])	$160.
958(2181)	.25L	Pewter	Hunter resting, signed Schlitt (master is 955[2180])	$160.
959(2177)	.25L	Pewter	Knight resting, signed Schlitt (master is 954[2176])	$160.

Number	Size	Lid	Description	Value
960(2177)	.25L	Pewter	Jester resting, signed Schlitt (master is 954[2176])	$160.
961(2179)	.25L	Pewter	Gnomes under bottle, signed Schlitt (master is 956[2178])	$160.
962(2179)	.25L	Pewter	Gnomes drinking, signed Schlitt (master is 956[2178])	$160.
966(2184)	.3L	Inlay	Gnomes drinking, by Schlitt (master is 953[2183] mate to 967)	$250.
966(2184)	.5L	Inlay		$285.
967(2184)	.3L	Inlay	Gnomes drinking, by Schlitt (master is 953[2183], mate to 966)	$250.
967(2184)	.5L	Inlay		$285.
979(1909)	.5L	Pewter	School in East Africa	$400.
980(1909)	.5L	Pewter	Miner	$300.
981(2271)	.5L	Pewter	Rowing race	$275.
983(1909)	.5L	Pewter	Falstaff	$275.
983(1526)	3.0L	Pewter		$375.

955(2271) .5L, 981(2271) .5L, 1055(2271) .5L

979(1909) .5L, 983(1909) .5L, 993(1909) .5L

Number	Size	Lid	Description	Value
993(1909)	.5L	Pewter	Drummers, signed Schlitt	$285.
994(2271)	.5L	Pewter	Soldiers drinking, signed Schlitt	$275.
994(2270)	3.3L	Pewter		$650.
1008(1909)	.5L	Pewter	Singer, signed Schlitt	$285.

960(2177) .25L, 1009(1909) .5L, 1010(1909) .5L

Number	Size	Lid	Description	Value
1009(1909)	.5L	Pewter	Gnomes working at wine press, by Schlitt (mate to 1010, matches bowls 2339/1028 and 2280/1005)	$175.
1010(1909)	.5L	Pewter	Gnomes drinking by Schlitt (mate to 1009, matches bowls 2339/1028 and 2280/1005)	$175.
1012(2261)	2.25L	Pewter	Drinking scene, signed Schlitt	$550.
1014(2262)	4.2L	Pewter	Munich Child and parading beer steins, signed Schlitt	$800.

1014(2262) 4.2L, 994(2270) 3.3L

Number	Size	Lid	Description	Value
1020(2271)	.5L	Pewter	Large group of people and verse, signed CK	$250.
1021(1909)	.5L	Pewter	Man and woman, signed CK	$275.
1022(2348)	3.3L	Pewter	Musician, man, and woman (master to steins and beakers 1023, 1024, 1025)	$300.
1023(2349)	.3L	Pewter	Fiddler (master is 1022 and matches beaker 1023[2327])	$150.

955(2180) 3.3L

702(1526) 3.0L

1012(2261) 2.25L, 1036(2384) 2.25L   1035(2384) 2.25L

Number	Size	Lid	Description	Value
1024(2349)	.3L	Pewter	Flute player (master is 1022 and matches beaker 1024[2327])	$150.
1025(2349)	.3L	Pewter	Barmaid (master is 1022 and matches beaker 1025[2327])	$150.
1027(2262)	4.2L	Pewter	4F motif, athletes	$775.
1031(2332)	2.7L	Pewter	Gnomes drinking, by Schlitt (master to 1032 and 1033[2333], beakers 1032 and 1033 [2368], matches coaster set 1032)	$250.
1032(2333)	.3L	Pewter	Gnomes drinking, by Schlitt (mate to 1033, master is 1031[2332], matches beaker 1032 [2368])	$150.

1037(1909) .5L, 1038(1909) .5L, 1042(1909) .5L

Number	Size	Lid	Description	Value
1033(2333)	.3L	Pewter	Gnomes drinking, by Schlitt (mate to 1032, master is 1031[2332], matches beaker 1033 [2368])	$150.
1035(2384)	2.25L	Pewter	Musical scene	$475.
1036(2384)	2.25L	Pewter	Musical scene, signed CK	$475.
1037(1909)	.5L	Pewter	Girl on bicycle, signed CK	$300.
1038(1909)	.5L	Pewter	Frogs drinking, signed Schlitt	$350.
1038(1526)	3.0L	Pewter		$475.
1041(2419)	4.15L	Pewter	Drunken judges, signed Schlitt	$850.
1042(1909)	.5L	Pewter	Man and woman with large key, signed Schlitt	$275.
1047(2140)	.5L	Pewter	Gnomes smoking	$275.
1054(2262)	4.2L	Pewter	Gambrinus and his followers	$850.

Number	Size	Lid	Description	Value
1055(2271)	.5L	Pewter	Drunken men in beer cellar	$275.
1055(2176)	2.7L	Pewter		$600.
1059(2488)	4.8L	Pewter	Humorous scene of steins, dice, and cards	$800.
1073(1909)	.5L	Pewter	Hunter, signed Schlitt	$275.
1074(1909)	.5L	Pewter	Peasant smoking pipe, signed Schlitt	$275.
1074(1526)	1.0L	Pewter		$325.
1075(2384)	2.25L	Pewter	Firefighting scenes	$700.
1076(1526)	.5L	Pewter	Marksman, signed Schlitt	$170.
1077(1526)	.5L	Pewter	Old man, signed Schlitt	$170.
1078(1526)	.5L	Pewter	Cavalier, signed Schlitt	$170.

954(2176) 2.7L, 1055(2176) 2.7L

1077(1526) .5L, 1078(1526) .5L, 1098(1526) .5L

1075(2384) 2.25L

1041(2419) 4.15L

Number	Size	Lid	Description	Value
1084(2177)	.25L	Pewter	Children eating and drinking (matches bowl 2595/1072)	$165.
1085(2177)	.25L	Pewter	Children eating and drinking (matches bowl 2595/1072)	$165.
1097(1909)	.5L	Pewter	Two drunks in front of inn	$275.
1098(1526)	.5L	Pewter	Soldiers drinking, U.S. German, Russian, and others	$250.
1101(1526)	.5L	Pewter	Barmaid	$175.
1102(1909)	.5L	Pewter	Drinking scene	$275.
1106(2488)	4.8L	Pewter	Seven Swabians, signed Schlitt (master to 1107)	$850.
1107(2271)	.5L	Pewter	Seven Swabians, signed Schlitt (master is 1106)	$325.
1108(1526)	.5L	Pewter	Ram and dancers, signed Schlitt	$175.
1108(1526)	1.0L	Pewter		$300.

1073(1909) .5L, 1074(1526) 1.0L, 1102(1909) .5L

Number	Size	Lid	Description	Value
1109(1909)	.5L	Pewter	Musicians, signed Schlitt (mate to 1110 and matches beaker 1109[2368])	$275.
1109(1526)	1.0L	Pewter		$325.
1110(1909)	.5L	Pewter	Soldiers drinking, signed Schlitt (mate to 1109 and matches beaker 1109[2368])	$285.
1110(1526)	1.0L	Pewter		$325.
1114(1526)	.5L	Pewter	Munich Child and *Hofbrauhaus*	$200.
1114(1526)	1.0L	Pewter		$325.
1128(2702)	4.8L	Pewter	Fat man and barmaid	$700.
1133(1909)	.5L	Pewter	People in conversation	$275.
1133(2488)	4.8L	Pewter		$700.
1143(1909)	.5L	Pewter	Tavern scene, signed Schlitt	$285.
1143(1526)	1.0L	Pewter		$325.
1143(2384)	2.25L	Pewter		$600.

1114(1526) 1.0L, 1108(1526) 1.0L, 1143(1909) .5L

1176(1909) .5L, 1177(1909) .5L, 1178(1909) .5L

Number	Size	Lid	Description	Value
		Set of Six		
1176(1909)	.5L	Pewter	Games (matches beaker 1176[2327])	$300.
1177(1909)	.5L	Pcwter	Music (matches beaker 1177[2327])	$300.
1178(1909)	.5L	Pewter	Beer (matches beaker 1178[2327])	$300.
1179(1909)	.5L	Pewter	Song (matches beaker 1179[2327])	$300.
1180(1909)	.5L	Pewter	Dance (matches beaker 1180[2327])	$300.
1181(1909)	.5L	Pewter	Love(matches beaker 1179[2327])	$300.
1195(1526)	.5L	Pewter	Art nouveau, floral design	$175.
1196(1909)	.5L	Pewter	Art nouveau, floral design	$200.
1197(2893)	2.4L	Pewter	Fisherman (master to beakers 1187 to 1192[2327])	$275.
1197(2893)	3.25L	Pewter		$325.

1197(2893) 3.25L

1200(2893) 3.25L

Number	Size	Lid	Description	Value
1200(2893)	3.25L	Pewter	Prussian eagle and city crests (master to 1200 series beakers)	$375.
1212(1909)	.5L	Pewter	Man bowling	$275.
1218(1526)	.5L	Pewter	Town scene of Heidelberg	$200.
1219(1526)	.5L	Pewter	Student	$175.
1237(1526)	.5L	Pewter	Dutch children	$200.
1280(3185)	.5L	Inlay	Round shaped, dancing scene	$225.
1282(1526)	.5L	Pewter	Hunter and peasant	$175.
1288(1909)	.5L	Pewter	Fox in formal clothes, eating and drinking	$300.
1290A(2893)	3.25L	Pewter	State crest of Prussia (matches beaker 1290A[2327])	$450.

Number	Size	Lid	Description	Value
1290B(2893)	3.25L	Pewter	State crest of Wurttemberg (matches beaker 1290B[2327])	$400.
1290C(2893)	3.25L	Pewter	State crest of Bavaria (matches beaker 1290C[2327])	$400.
1290D(2893)	3.25L	Pewter	State crest of Saxony (matches beaker 1290D [2327])	$425.
1290E(2893)	3.25L	Pewter	State crest of Hesse (matches beaker 1290E [2327])	$400.
1290F(2893)	3.25L	Pewter	State crest of Baden (matches beaker 1290F [2327])	$400.
1302(2893)	3.25L	Pewter	American eagle (matches beaker 1302 [2327])	$400.

1290D(2893) 3.25L

1302(2893) 3.25L

1338(3257) 1.65L

Number	Size	Lid	Description	Value
1338(3257)	1.65L	Pewter	Singing frogs	$375.
1502(1526)	.5L	Inlay	Military figure	$150.
7201(1526)	.5L	Pewter	Man with stein	$175.
7202(1526)	.5L	Pewter	Man with stein	$175.

1288(1909) .5L

1280(3185) .5L

7201(1526) .5L

7202(1526) .5L

*Some print under glaze steins do not have decoration numbers, the
following are some of these:*

Number	Size	Lid	Description	Value
		German Places:		
(2140)	.5L	Pewter	*Mettlach* hospital, Christmas, seen with dates from 1917 to 1920	$600.
(1526)	.5L	Pewter	Town scene of Trier	$150.
(2140)	.5L	Pewter	Town scene of Thorn	$250.
		United States Places:		
(2140)	.5L	Pewter	*Newport* souvenir	$275.
(2140)	.5L	Pewter	*Narragansett* souvenir	$275.
(1909)	.5L	Pewter	Coat of arms of *St. Augustine, Florida*	$300.

(1909) *St. Augustine* .5L, (2140) *Narragansett* .5L, (2140) *Newport* .5L

Number	Size	Lid	Description	Value
		Universities:		
(1909)	.5L	Inlay	*Universitat Halle, Wittenberg*	$225.
(2222)	.5L	Inlay	*Signature stein,* signatures of 48 members attending *75th Annual Founder's Day meeting, July 27, 1895,* of the Saxo-Borussia, a Heidelberg student association	$350.
(1526)	.5L	Pewter	*Yale University* student	$175.
(1909)	.5L	Pewter	*Yale University* student	$250.
(2140)	.5L	Pewter	College sport scenes, football and baseball, known to exist for Harvard, Yale, Brown, and Princeton	$350.
(2140)	.5L	Pewter	*Harvard University,* with two bicycle scenes	$400.

(1526) *Yale* .5L, (1909) *Yale* .5L   (2222) *Signature Stein* .5L

(2140) College sport scenes .5L

Number	Size	Lid	Description	Value
		Breweries:		
(1909)	.5L	Inlay	*Bartholomay's Brewing Co.*	$150.
(1526)	.5L	Pewter	*E. Tosetti Brewing Co.*	$175.
(2140)	.5L	Pewter	*E. Tosetti Brewing Co.*	$225.

(2140) *Tosetti* .5L, (1526) *Tosetti* .5L, (2303) *Bartholomay's* 3'' tall, (1909) *Bartholomay's* .5L

Number	Size	Lid	Description	Value
(1526)	1.0L	Inlay	*Quilmes Brewery*	$200.
(1909)	.5L	Pewter	*Pilsner Export Beer New York-Chicago*	$225.
(1909)	.5L	Pewter	*Export Lager, Keeley Brewing Co., Chicago Illinois*	$150.

(1909) *Pilsner* .5L, (1526) *Baumeister Verein* .5L, (1909) *Export* .5L

Number	Size	Lid	Description	Value
		Other Decorations:		
(1526)	.5L	Inlay	*Baumeister Verein von New York und Umgegend, 1891-1906*	$175.
(3095)	.5L	None	*Hires Root Beer*	$100.
(2893)	1.0L	Pewter	*Hires Root Beer*	$350.
(1526)	.5L	Pewter	Keeper of wine cellar	$175.
(1526)	1.0L	Pewter	Munich Child, Prussian eagle, and 4F motif	$350.
(1526)	.5L	Inlay	Prussian eagle and 4F motif, *1908 Turnfest*	$250.
(2152)	.5L	Inlay	Frederick III	$300.

Number	Size	Lid	Description	Value
(2140)	.5L	Pewter	*Legion of American Wheelmen,* two bicycle scenes	$400.
(1526)	.5L	Pewter	Elk's Club (matches stein [2893] and beaker [2327])	$175.
(2893)	3.25L	Pewter	Elk's Club (matches stein [1526] and beaker [2327])	$275.
		Miniatures:		
(2303)	2½'' tall	None	*Howland Jeweler, New Bedford, Massachusetts*	$100.
(2303)	2½'' tall	None	*The Shriners and Bartholomay's Brewing Co., Rochester, New York, July 1911*	$80.
(2303)	3'' tall	Pewter	*Bartholomay's Brewing Co.*	$120.

(1526) *1908 Turnfest* .5L, (1526) Munich Child 1.0L, (1526) Elk's Club .5L

(2140) *Legion of American Wheelmen* .5L

5. Plaques

Although listed in the original Mettlach catalogs as *Schalen,* or dishes, it is unlikely that these wares were often used for other than wall decorations. Thus the term *plaque* seems more appropriate. Because these plaques have a decorated surface area that is relatively larger than that of steins, and because the decoration can be viewed all at once, many collectors feel the plaques exemplify the finest of Mettlach quality.

Mettlach plaques were made using all of the various production techniques described in Chapter 2. The plaques are all listed sequentially according to the incised mold numbers, except the 5000-series plaques which are listed by decoration number. All PUG plaques were made using the blank plaque with mold number 1044; they can thus be found listed under that number, even though occasionally this incised mark may not appear.

The 5000-series plaques are generally decorated with blue and white colors, resembling Delftware. These Mettlach Delft-type plaques seem to have been produced by print under glaze techniques, but all were, in fact, hand painted. The most common scenes on the Delft plaques are windmills, sailboats, and seashores. A general price range for the various sizes can be found at the beginning of the 5000 numbers, followed by specific examples.

Number	Size*	Type	Description	Value
834	13"	Relief	Gargoyles, flowers, nude girl	$275.
852	12"	Mosaic & Etched	Pan with flute	$250.
864	10"	Mosaic & Etched	Nude girl with butterflies	$250.
875	11"	Etched	Geometric design, pie crust border	$150.
886	12½"	Etched	Geometric design	$175.

*Measurement is diameter for round plaques, unless noted.

852

Number	Size	Type	Description	Value
894	13½"	Etched	Geometric design (mate to 1706)	$175.
895	12½"	Etched	Cherub and griffin	$275.

1044 Various sized plaques were made with this number (1044); generally they carried print under glaze scenes that were identified by decoration numbers. Among the most numerous of these scenes are the castle scenes, generally found in 17", 14", and 12" sizes. They sell, except for a few exceptions, for $250 to $325 (17"), $135 to $175 (14"), and $100 to $125 (12"). Some examples (including exceptions) are listed below with the decoration number following the mold number.

1044/126

1044/127

1044/159

1044/162

1044/190

Number	Size	Type	Description	Value
1044/80	17"	PUG	Cavalier (mate to 81)	$600.
1044/81	17"	PUG	Cavalier (mate to 80)	$600.
1044/92	14"	PUG	City hall of Berncastle	$160.
1044/126	17"	PUG	Dog (mate to 127)	$250.
1044/127	17"	PUG	Dog (mate to 126)	$250.
1044/159	12"	PUG	Kaub on Rhine	$100.
1044/162	14"	PUG	*Niederwalden Kmal*	$300.
1044/170	17½"	PUG	Deer (mate to 171)	$250.
1044/171	17½"	PUG	Deer (mate to 170)	$250.
1044/172	12"	PUG	Wartburg	$125.
1044/190	12"	PUG	Stuttgart	$100.
1044/221	14"	PUG	*Munchen* (mate to 222)	$300.
1044/222	14"	PUG	*Nurnberg* (mate to 221)	$300.

1044/221, 1044/222

1044/263, 1044/264

Number	Size	Type	Description	Value
1044/263	17½''	PUG	Lohengrin in boat, castle and people in background (mate to 264)	$575.
1044/264	17½''	PUG	Lohengrin on shore, castle and people in background (mate to 263)	$575.
1044/411	14''	PUG	Barmaid drinking (mate to 412)	$375.
1044/411	17½''	PUG		$500.
1044/412	14''	PUG	Postman drinking (mate to 411)	$375.
1044/412	17½''	PUG		$500.

1044/991, 1044/992

1044/1014

1044/1099

Number	Size	Type	Description	Value
1044/991	7½"	PUG	Gnomes picking grapes	$150.
1044/992	7½"	PUG	Gnomes carrying grapes	$150.
1044/1014	17½"	PUG	Munich Child and steins walking, signed Schlitt (matches steins 2767, 1014[2262], beaker 1014[2368])	$700.

1044/1066, 1044/1067

1044/1104, 1044/1105

Number	Size	Type	Description	Value
1044/1066	17½"	PUG	Water pump and geese, signed Reils (mate to 1067)	$450.
1044/1067	17½"	PUG	Old farmhouse, signed Reils (mate to 1066)	$450.
1044/1099	17½"	PUG	Young girl and two young boys, signed Reils	$475.
1044/1104	17"	PUG	Farm, woman, geese (mate to 1105)	$450.

1044/1122, 1044/1123

Number	Size	Type	Description	Value
1044/1105	17"	PUG	Farm, man, woman, goats (mate to 1104)	$450.
1044/1122	17"	PUG	Young girl and geese (mate to 1123)	$500.
1044/1123	17"	PUG	Young girl and geese (mate to 1122)	$500.
1044/1143	17"	PUG	Cavaliers drinking (mate to 1144)	$600.
1044/1144	17"	PUG	Tavern scene, signed Schlitt (mate to 1143)	$650.
1044/1205	17½"	PUG	Cavaliers drinking (mate to 1206)	$600.
1044/1206	17½"	PUG	Drinking scene (mate to 1205)	$600.

1044/1143, 1044/1144

Number	Size	Type	Description	Value
1044/6123	19"	Rookwood	Woman's portrait (mate to 6124)	$500.
1044/6124	19"	Rookwood	Woman's portrait (mate to 6123)	$500.
1044/6125	14"	Rookwood	Woman's portrait (mate to 6126)	$400.
1044/6126	14"	Rookwood	Woman's portrait (mate to 6125)	$400.
1044	17½"	PUG	Jesus Christ	$700.
1044	17"	PUG	Konigsburger castle	$300.
1044	17"	PUG	Marienburg	$300.

1044/1205, 1044 Jesus Christ

1048/3036II, 1048/3036IV

Number	Size	Type	Description	Value
		Set of Six		
1048/3036I	16"	Etched	Baptism	$650.
1048/3036II	16"	Etched	Opening crypt of Carl the Great by order of Otto III	$650.
1048/3036III	16"	Etched	Carl the Great gives crown to his son Ludwig	$650.
1048/3036IV	16"	Etched	Destroying the *Irmensaule* by Paderborn	$650.

Number	Size	Type	Description	Value
1048/3036V	16"	Etched	Crowning of Carl the Great by Pope Leo III	$650.
1048/3036VI	16"	Etched	Building the Aachen *Munsters*	$650.
1091/3061	21"	Etched	Three lions	$1200.
1094/3062	16½"	Etched	Self-portrait of Titian	$600.
1097/3063	16½"	Etched	Mary and Christ	$600.
1106/3096	17"	Etched	Three men running in forest	$650.
1107/3091	14½"	Etched	Cherubs	$550.

1091/3061

1106/3096, 1109/3092

Number	Size	Type	Description	Value
1108	17"	Etched	Castle scene(mate to 1365)	$900.
1109/3092	17½"	Etched	Portrait of Bismarck	$700.
1110/3093	15"	Relief & Etched (Glazed)	Nymphs	$500.
1165/3095	14"	Etched	Flowers	$200.
1168	17"	Etched (Glazed)	Bearded man with fancy hat, signed Warth (mate is 1411)	$675.
1170/3097	21"	Etched (Glazed)	Flowers	$350.

1108, 1365

Number	Size	Type	Description	Value
1172/3098	17"	Etched (Glazed)	Birds and flowers	$350.
1173/3099	24½"	Etched (Glazed)	Parrots and trees	$500.
1176/3094	21"	Etched	Geometric design and flowers	$400.
1178	17"	Etched (Glazed) & PUG	Flowers and girl's portrait	$400.
1182/4005	11"	Etched	Geometric design	$150.
1183/4006	16"	Etched (Glazed)	Birds and flowers	$350.

1411, 1168

Number	Size	Type	Description	Value
1245	13"	Etched	Geometric design	$200.
1259	10"	Etched	Geometric design	$125.
1260	11"	Etched	Geometric design (mate to 1685)	$175.
1285	13"	Etched	Dove and geometric design	$350.
1294	18"	Etched	Geometric design	$350.
1364	17"	Etched (Glazed) & PUG	Flowers and girl's portrait	$400.
1365	17"	Etched	Castle scene (mate to 1108)	$900.
1369	11"	Etched	Bird in center panel and geometric design	$225.
1371	8"	Etched	Geometric design	$150.
1372	9"	Etched	Geometric design	$100.

1405, 1376

1384, 1385

Number	Size	Type	Description	Value
1374	8"	Etched	Geometric design	$150.
1376	11"	Etched	Woman's portrait (mate to 1405)	$325.
1384	14½"	Etched	Knight carrying flag, signed Schultz (mate to 1385)	$800.
1385	14½"	Etched	Knight carrying weapon, signed Schultz (mate to 1384)	$800.

1386

1387   1388

Number	Size	Type	Description	Value
1386	20"	Etched & Relief	*Germania,* border is medallions of German cities	$2500.
1387	11"	Etched	Knight (mate to 1388)	$375.
1388	11"	Etched	Knight (mate to 1387)	$375.
1391	9½"	Etched	Geometric design	$150.
1392	9½"	Etched	Geometric design	$175.
1404	22"	Etched	Geometric design	$450.
1405	11"	Etched	Woman's portrait (mate to 1376)	$325.
1407	7½"	Etched	Birds in flight	$200.
1408	5½"	Etched	Geometric design	$125.
1410	35"	Etched	Man with fancy hat (mate to 1490)	$2800.
1411	17"	Etched (Glazed)	Woman with fancy hat (mate to 1168)	$675.

1425, 1424

1474

1422

Number	Size	Type	Description	Value
1412	7½"	Etched	Bird on branch	$200.
1413	7½"	Etched	Crane in water	$200.
1414	11½"	Etched	Bird in tree (mate to 1415)	$325.
1415	11½"	Etched	Bird in tree (mate to 1414)	$325.
1417	7½"	Etched	Crane in water	$200.
1418	19½"	Etched	Bird in flowers (mate to 1676)	$550.
1422	14½"	Etched	Black horse (mate to 1423)	$600.
1423	14½"	Etched	White horse (mate to 1422)	$600.
1424	16"	Etched	Woman in fancy hat signed Warth (mate to 1425)	$500.
1425	16"	Etched	Woman in fancy hat, signed Warth (mate to 1424, same scene as 1549)	$500.

Set of Four

Number	Size	Type	Description	Value
1473	17"x11"	Etched	Woman picking flowers, signed Warth	$1100.
1474	17"x11"	Etched	Woman watering flowers, signed Warth	$1100.

Number	Size	Type	Description	Value
1488	17"x11"	Etched	Woman holding flowers, signed Warth	$1100.
1489	17"x11"	Etched	Woman picking grapes, signed Warth	$1100.
1490	35"	Etched	Woman in fancy hat (mate to 1410)	$2800.
1495	16½"	Etched	Birds and flowers (mate to 1682)	$500.
1500	15"	Relief	Two swans in lake, relief in full color (mate to 1677)	$450.
1549	9"x9"	Etched	Woman in fancy hat (same scene as 1425)	$300.
1607	12"	Etched	Barefoot girl carrying basket (part of set 1651, 1652)	$350.
1617	16½"	Relief	Woman with butterfly wings on branch, full color relief (mate to 1696)	$750.
1651	12"	Etched	Barefoot girl carrying basket (part of set 1607, 1652)	$350.
1652	12"	Etched	Barefoot girl carrying basket (part of set 1607, 1651)	$350.
1676	19½"	Etched	Flowers (mate to 1418)	$550.

1495, 1682

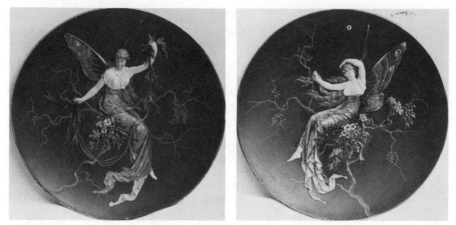

1696, 1617

Number	Size	Type	Description	Value
1677	15"	Relief	Two birds and pond, full color relief (mate to 1500)	$450.
1682	16½"	Etched	Birds and flowers (mate to 1495)	$500.
1685	11"	Mosaic	Geometric design (mate to 1260)	$175.
1688	9"	Etched	Geometric design	$150.
1694	10"	Etched	Geometric design	$150.
1696	16½"	Relief	Woman with butterfly wings on branch, full color relief (mate to 1617)	$750.
1706	13½"	Mosaic	Geometric design (mate to 894)	$175.

1651, 1607, 1652

1769, 1770

Number	Size	Type	Description	Value
1769	15''	Etched	Battle scene with Arnold von Winkelried, signed Schultz (mate to 1770)	$1700.
1770	15''	Etched	William Tell after shooting apple, signed Schultz (mate to 1769)	$1700.

2013

Number	Size	Type	Description	Value
2010	12½"x10½"	Etched	Rampant lion, shield shaped (mate to 2011)	$750.
2011	12½"x10½"	Etched	Imperial eagle, shield shaped (mate to 2010)	$750.
2013	27½"	Etched	Imperial eagle surrounded by fourteen city crests	$8500.
2022	20"	Etched & Relief	Young man playing lute, border is floral relief in full color (mate to 2023)	$650.
2023	20"	Etched & Relief	Young man, border is floral relief in full color (mate to 2022)	$650.

2042, 2041

Number	Size	Type	Description	Value
2041	15"	Etched	Man and woman on horseback, jumping fence, signed Stocke (mate to 2042)	$950.
2042	15"	Etched	Man and woman on horseback, signed Stocke (mate to 2041)	$950.
2070	15"	Etched	Two dogs harassing stag, signed Stocke (mate to 2071)	$700.
2071	15"	Etched	Three dogs attacking boar, signed Stocke (mate to 2070)	$700.

2070, 2071

2113, 2112

2149, 2148

Number	Size	Type	Description	Value
2078	15"	Etched	Two Ulans on horseback on snow-covered field, signed Stocke (mate to 2079 part of set of eight military plaques)	$1150.
2079	15"	Etched	Four Dragoons on horseback, signed Stocke (mate to 2078, part of set of eight military plaques)	$1250.
2080	15"	Etched	Four Curissairs on horseback, signed Stocke (mate to 2081, part of set of eight military plaques)	$1250.
2081	15"	Etched	Four Husars on horseback, signed Stocke (mate to 2080, part of set of eight military plaques)	$1150.
2112	16"	Etched	Gnome in tree, holding two bottles, signed Schlitt (mate to 2113, matches stein 2134)	$1600.
2113	16"	Etched	Gnome in tree, drinking from mug, signed Schlitt (mate to 2112, matches stein 2133)	$1600.
2142	15"	Etched	Bismarck on horseback, signed Stocke (mate to 2143, part of set of eight military plaques)	$1000.
2143	15"	Etched	Von Moltke on horseback, signed Stocke (mate to 2142, part of set of eight military plaques)	$1000.

Number	Size	Type	Description	Value
2146	15"	Etched	Infantry men shooting rifles, signed Stocke (mate to 2147, part of set of eight military plaques)	$1100.
2147	15"	Etched	Artillery men moving cannons, signed Stocke (mate to 2146, part of set of eight military plaques)	$1100.
2148	16"	Etched	Snow White and Seven Dwarfs, signed Schlitt (mate to 2149)	$1800.
2149	16"	Etched	Papageno playing flute, signed Schlitt (mate to 2148)	$1700.

2188, 2187

Number	Size	Type	Description	Value
2187	17½"	Etched	Knight on horseback, House of *Hohenzollern,* gold background (mate to 2188)	$3200.
2188	17½"	Etched	Knight on horseback, House of *Habsburg,* gold background (mate to 2187)	$3200.

2078, 2079

2080, 2081

Number	Size	Type	Description	Value
2195	17½''	Etched	Castle on cliff, Rheinstein (mate to 2196)	$900.
2196	17½''	Etched	Castle on cliff, Stolzenfels (mate to 2195)	$900.
2199	15½''	Etched	Greek soldier playing lyre for maiden, Etruscan style, signed Schlitt (mate to 2200)	$1100.

2142, 2143

2146, 2147

Number	Size	Type	Description	Value
2200	15½''	Etched	Pan playing flute for maiden, Etruscan style, signed Schlitt (mate to 2199)	$1100.
2287	17½''	Etched	Two knights shaking hands, signed Quidenus (mate to 2288)	$1300.
2288	17½''	Etched	Knight and lady walking in garden, signed Quidenus (mate to 2287)	$1300.

2195, 2196

2199, 2200

Number	Size	Type	Description	Value
2322	15''	Etched	Knight trying to kiss maiden, being pushed away (mate to 2323, same scene as 2647 and stein 2381)	$850.
2323	15''	Etched	Knight is being kissed by maiden, after returning from battle (mate to 2322, same scene as 2648 and stein 2381)	$850.

Number	Size	Type	Description	Value
2350	17"	Etched	Flowers (mate to 2351)	$400.
2351	17"	Etched	Flowers (mate to 2350)	$400.
2361A	17½"	Etched	Wartburg castle (mate to 2361B)	$900.
2361B	17½"	Etched	Wartburg castle (mate to 2361A)	$900.
2362	17½"	Etched	Heidelburg castle	$900.
2442	19"	Cameo	Trojan warriors on boat, signed Stahl (mate to 2443)	$1000.
2443	19"	Cameo	Trojan lady and her servants, signed Stahl (mate to 2442)	$1000.

2287, 2288

2322, 2323

2350, 2351

Number	Size	Type	Description	Value
2444	11"	Cameo	Oval shaped, children playing musical instruments and singing (mate to 2445)	$300.
2445	11"	Cameo	Oval shaped, children playing musical instruments and singing (mate to 2444)	$300.
2459	19"	Etched	Hamburg crest (mate to 2460)	$1800.
2460	19"	Etched	Stuttgart crest (mate to 2459)	$1800.
2484	12"	Etched	Knight on white horse (mate to 2485)	$750.
2485	12"	Etched	Maiden on white horse (mate to 2484)	$750.

2484, 2485

2361A, 2361B

2362

2442, 2443

2507, 2508

Number	Size	Type	Description	Value
2507	17½''	Etched	Art nouveau, mermaid on large shell in pond, holding baby, signed Hein (mate to 2508)	$700.
2508	17½''	Etched	Art nouveau, mermaid on large shell in pond, signed Hein (mate to 2507)	$700.

2459

2518

Number	Size	Type	Description	Value
2513	16"x9½"	Etched	Rectangular, young boy and girl looking at festive table (mate to 2546)	$1100.
2517	17½"	Etched	Town scene of Konigstein (mate to 2518)	$950.
2518	17½"	Etched	Town scene of Meissen (mate to 2517)	$950.
2533	17½"	Etched	Godesburg castle (mate to 2534)	$950.
2534	17½"	Etched	Drachenfels castle (mate to 2533)	$950.

2533, 2534

Number	Size	Type	Description	Value
2541	16"	Etched	Art nouveau, girl's portrait, signed Thevenin (mate to 2542)	$700.
2542	16"	Etched	Art nouveau, girl's portrait, signed Thevenin (mate to 2541)	$700.
2543	16½"	Etched	Branch of tree (mate to 2606)	$350.

Number	Size	Type	Description	Value
2544	19½"	Etched	Art nouveau, girl's portrait (mate to 2545)	$800.
2545	19½"	Etched	Art nouveau, girl's portrait (mate to 2544)	$800.
2546	16"x9½"	Etched	Rectangular, young girl reclined in bed of flowers, signed Mangum (mate to 2513)	$1100.
2548	17½"	Etched	Art nouveau, girl's portrait (mate to 2549)	$500.
2549	17½"	Etched	Art nouveau, girl's portrait (mate to 2548)	$500.
2550	18½"	Etched	Bird in flight over barren mountain landscape (mate to 2551)	$700.
2551	18½"	Etched	Bird in flight over barren mountain landscape, with moonlight (mate to 2550)	$700.
2558	16"	Etched	Flowers, with geometric background (mate to 2559)	$450.
2559	16"	Etched	Flowers, with geometric background (mate to 2558)	$450.

2560, 2561

2563, 2564

Number	Size	Type	Description	Value
2560	17½''	Etched	Dogwood trees (mate to 2561)	$575.
2561	17½''	Etched	Dogwood trees (mate to 2560)	$575.
2563	17½''	Etched	Man and woman riding bicycles at night (mate to 2564)	$1850.
2564	17½''	Etched	Man and woman riding bicycles in day-time (mate to 2563)	$1850.
2590	15''	Etched	Young girl rolling hoop (mate to 2591)	$700.
2591	15''	Etched	Young girl jumping rope (mate to 2590)	$700.
2592	17½''	Etched	Owl in tree (mate to 2593)	$650.
2593	17½''	Etched	Hawk in tree (mate to 2592)	$650.
2596	16''	Etched	Art nouveau, girl's portrait (mate to 2597)	$675.
2597	16''	Etched	Art nouveau, girl's portrait (mate to 2596)	$675.
2606	16½''	Etched	Branch of tree (mate to 2543)	$350.

2590, 2591

2542

2596, 2597

2621, 2622, 2623

Number	Size	Type	Description	Value
		Set of Six		
2621	7½''	Etched	Cavalier pouring wine, by Quidenus	$250.
2622	7½''	Etched	Cavalier holding glass, signed Quidenus	$250.
2623	7½''	Etched	**Waiter serving wine, by** Quidenus	$250.
2624	7½''	Etched	Cavalier smoking pipe and drinking, signed Quidenus	$250.
2625	7½''	Etched	Cavalier playing mandolin, by Quidenus	$250.
2626	7½''	Etched	Cavalier drinking from stein, signed Quidenus (this set matches beakers 1091 to 1096 [2368] and coasters 2817 to 2822)	$250.

Coaster 2819, Plaque 2624, Beaker 1095(2368)

Number	Size	Type	Description	Value
2644	18½"	Etched	Two owls in cave (mate to 2645)	$750.
2645	18½"	Etched	Two eagles on mountain (mate to 2644)	$750.
2647	9"	Etched	Knight trying to kiss maiden, being pushed away (mate to 2648, same scene as 2322 and stein 2381)	$325.
2648	9"	Etched	Knight being kissed by maiden, after returning from battle (mate to 2647, same scene as 2323 and stein 2381)	$325.

2644, 2645

Number	Size	Type	Description	Value
2658	16½"	Etched	Swimming fish (mate to 2659)	$400.
2659	16½"	Etched	Swimming fish (mate to 2658)	$400.
2680	21½"	Relief & Hand Painted	Art nouveau, woman's portrait, irregularly shaped border (mate to 2689)	$800.

2697, 2698

Number	Size	Type	Description	Value
2689	21½"	Relief & Hand Painted	Art nouveau, woman's portrait, irregularly shaped border (mate to 2680)	$800.
2697	17"	Etched	Dwarf eating porridge in field of mushrooms, signed Schlitt (mate to 2698)	$3800.
2698	17"	Etched	Dwarf reading book in field of mushrooms, signed Schlitt (mate to 2697)	$3800.
2712	9½"	Etched	Black Forest scene with girl (mate to 2713)	$200.
2713	9½"	Etched	Black Forest scene with girl (mate to 2712)	$200.

2712, 2713

2739

2740, 2741

Number	Size	Type	Description	Value
2739	19"	Etched (Glazed)	Munich Child in center oval, buildings of Munich in background	$2500.
2740	18½"	Etched	Running Centaur holding baby Centaur, running with dog (mate to 2741)	$1400.
2741	18½"	Etched	Centaur with bow and arrows, holding bird (mate to 2740)	$1400.

Number	Size	Type	Description	Value
2749	19"	Etched	Scene of stream and trees, church in background (mate to 2750)	$900.
2750	19"	Etched	Large sailing ship (mate to 2749)	$1000.
2759	17"	Etched	Town of Salzburg (mate to 2760)	$1000.
2760	17"	Etched	Town of Kufstein (mate to 2759)	$1000.

2759, 2760

2769, 2770

Number	Size	2794, 2795 Type	Description	Value
2769	18½''	Etched	Night scene with angel, signed Schlitt (mate to 2770)	$2000.
2770	18½''	Etched	Day scene with angel, signed Schlitt (mate to 2769)	$2000.
2794	17½''	Cameo	*Words of love* serenade scene (mate to 2795)	$950.
2795	17½''	Cameo	*Words of love* serenade scene (mate to 2794)	$950.

2804, 2805

Number	Size	Type	Description	Value
2804	15"	Etched	Deer (mate to 2805)	$700.
2805	15"	Etched	Deer (mate to 2804)	$700.
2874	18"	Cameo	Woman holding harp and torch, two other figures (mate to 2875)	$750.
2875	18"	Cameo	Woman holding banner, two other figures (mate to 2874)	$750.
2898	18"	Etched	Young girl with flowers, Spring scene (part of set with 2899, 2997, 2998)	$1200.

2874, 2875

Number	Size	Type	Description	Value
2899	18"	Etched	Young girl with wheat, Summer scene (part of set with 2898, 2997, 2998)	$1200.
2970	10½"	Cameo	Young girl with wings, holding dove (mate to 2971)	$275.
2971	10½"	Cameo	Young girl with wings, holding lyre (mate to 2970)	$275.

2898, 2899

2997

Number	Size	Type	Description	Value
2997	18''	Etched	Young girl picking fruit, Fall scene (part of set with 2898, 2899, 2998)	$1200.
2998	18''	Etched	Young girl in snow-covered field, Winter scene (part of set with 2898, 2899, 2997)	$1200.
3038	10½''	Cameo	Mythological man and woman (mate to 3039)	$275.
3039	10½''	Cameo	Roman man and woman (mate to 3038)	$275.

Number	Size	Type	Description	Value
3112	18''	Cameo	Four women, mytho-logical scene, geometric border	$850.
3161	17½''	Etched	Two cavaliers drinking one seated on cannon, one seated on barrel (mate to 3162)	$1200.
3162	17½''	Etched	Two cavaliers toasting (mate to 3161, same scene as stein 1932)	$1200.
		Set of Four		
3163	17½''	Etched	Lohengrin walking up to maiden	$1400.
3164	17½''	Etched	Maiden coming out of water, heading towards knight	$1400.
3165	17½''	Etched	Knight and maiden embracing, king in chair	$1350.
3166	17½''	Etched	Lohengrin's departure	$1500.
3182	17½''	Etched	Town of *Hohkonigsburg* (mate to 3183)	$900.
3183	17½''	Etched	Town of *Nurnberg* (mate to 3182)	$900.

3161, 3162

3163, 3164

3165, 3166

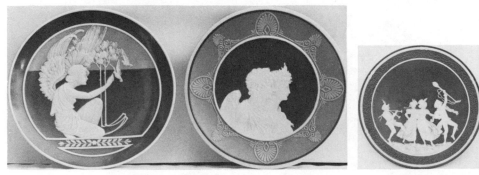

2970, 3038   3273

Number	Size	3182, 3183 Type	Description	Value
3225	13¼''x11''	PUG	Shield shaped, Elk's Club	$250.
3225	13¼''x11''	PUG	Shield shaped, United States	$450.
3225	13¼''x11''	PUG	Shield shaped, French Republic	$400.
3225	13¼''x11''	PUG	Shield shaped, Canada	$400.
3225	13¼''x11''	PUG	Shield shaped, Austria	$400.
3225	13¼''x11''	PUG	Shield shaped, Italy	$400.
3225	13¼''x11''	PUG	Shield shaped, England	$400.

Elk's Club   United States   French Republic

Prussian eagle with city crests

Munich

Dresden   Frankfurt   Hamburg

Number	Size	Type	Description	Value
3225	13¼"x11"	PUG	Shield shaped, Prussian eagle	$425.
3225	13¼"x11"	PUG	Shield shaped, Prussian eagle with city crests	$450.
3225	13¼"x11"	PUG	Shield shaped, Munich	$425.
3225	13¼"x11"	PUG	Shield shaped, Hannover	$375.
3225	13¼"x11"	PUG	Shield shaped, Dresden	$375.
3225	13¼"x11"	PUG	Shield shaped, Frankfurt	$375.
3225	13¼"x11"	PUG	Shield shaped, Hamburg	$375.
3225	13¼"x11"	PUG	Shield shaped, Berlin	$425.

Number	Size	Type	Description	Value
3225	13¼"x11"	PUG	Shield shaped plaques for other German cities	$375.
3272	6½"	Cameo	Four young girls dancing, signed Stahl (mate to 3273)	$300.
3273	6½"	Cameo	Two young men with musical instruments, dancing with two young girls, signed Stahl (mate to 3272)	$300.
3275	6"	Cameo	Octagon shaped, three ladies	$250.
5000's	8"	Delft	Windmill, sailboat or seashore scenes	$100.
5000's	10½"	Delft		$125.
5000's	12"	Delft		$150.
5000's	14"	Delft		$175.
5000's	17½"	Delft		$200.
5000's	13"x8"	Delft		$275.
5000's	16"x10"	Delft		$300.
5000's	17½"x11"	Delft		$350.
5000's	20"x13"	Delft		$400.
5000's	22"x14"	Delft		$425.
5000's	24"x15"	Delft		$450.
5009	14"	Delft	Portrait of woman	$175.
5010	14"	Delft	Crest and geometric design	$150.

5152, 5153 (8" diameter, value $100. each)

5126 (22''x14'', value $425.)

Number	Size	Type	Description	Value
5036	17½''	Delft	Town of Hannover	$250.
5037	17½''	Delft	*Martinskirsche* in Cologne (mate to 5038)	$250.
5038	17½''	Delft	Cologne city hall (mate to 5037)	$250.
5041	12''	Delft	Musician (mate to 5042)	$150.
5042	12''	Delft	Gentleman (mate to 5041)	$150.

5036

5038

5041, 5042

Number	Size	Type	Description	Value
		Set of Three		
5062	17½"	Delft	Town of Stuttgart	$275.
5063	17½"	Delft	Nurnberg castle	$275.
5064	17½"	Delft	Nurnberg marketplace	$275.
5065	8"	Delft	Nurnberg *Bratwurstglocklein*	$125.
5078	17½"	Delft	Town of Mettlach	$600.
5109	10"	Delft	Birds	$125.
5121	16"x10"	Delft	Rectangular, cherubs (mate to 5122)	$300.
5122	16"x10"	Delft	Rectangular, cherubs (mate to 5121)	$300.

5062, 5063

5134, 5176, 5177

Number	Size	Type	Description	Value
5123	22"x14"	Delft	Rectangular, cherubs (mate to 5124)	$400.
5124	22"x14"	Delft	Rectangular, cherubs (mate to 5123)	$400.
5132	17½"	Delft	*Andernach* (mate to 5133)	$250.
5133	17½"	Delft	*Pfalz bei Kaub* castle (mate to 5132)	$250.
5134	12"	Delft	*Andernach* (mate to 5135)	$175.
5135	12"	Delft	*Pfalz bei Kaub* castle (mate to 5134)	$175.
5163	17½"	Delft	Nurnberg artists	$350.
5164	17½"	Delft	Cochem castle (mate to 5165)	$250.
5165	17½"	Delft	Stolzenfels castle (mate to 5164)	$250.
5166	19"	Delft	Woman's portrait (mate to 5167)	$200.
5167	19"	Delft	Woman's portrait (mate to 5166)	$200.
5176	12"	Delft	Cochem castle (mate to 5177)	$175.
5177	12"	Delft	Stolzenfels castle (mate to 5176)	$175.
5182	14"	Delft	Man's portrait, after Franz Hals (mate to 5183)	$300.

Number	Size	Type	Description	Value
5183	14''	Delft	Man's portrait, after Franz Hals (mate to 5182)	$300.
5184	19''	Delft	Louis de Silvestre, after Raph. Mengs (mate to 5185)	$400.
5185	19''	Delft	William Burggraf, after Rembrandt (mate to 5184)	$400.
5218	22½''	Delft	Man's portrait, after Rembrandt (mate to 5219)	$500.
5219	22½''	Delft	Senator Holzschuher, after A. Durer (mate to 5218)	$500.

Set of Four

Number	Size	Type	Description	Value
5226	8''	Delft	Happy cavalier, after Franz Hals	$150.
5227	8''	Delft	Drinking cavalier	$150.
5228	8''	Delft.	Drinking cavalier, after Arie de Vois	$150.
5229	8''	Delft	Happy cavalier, after William Van Mieris	$150.

5185

Number	Size	Type	Description	Value
5230	26"x18½"	Delft & Relief	Happy cavaliers, after William Van Mieris, relief signed Stahl (mate to 5231)	$700.
5231	26"x18½"	Delft & Relief	Violinist, after Gerard Dou, relief signed Stahl (mate to 5230)	$700.

5231

Number	Size	Type	Description	Value
5334	17½"x11"	Brown Delft	Young boy and dog, hand painted, after Erelman (mate to 5335)	$1300.
5335	17½"x11"	Brown Delft	Young girl and dog, hand painted, after Erelman (mate to 5334)	$1300.

Number	Size	Type	Description	Value
6034	29"x19"	Natural Glazed	Young girl standing, ornate border (mate to 6035)	$1200.
6035	29"x19"	Natural Glazed	Young girl seated, ornate border (mate to 6034)	$1200.

5334, 5335

Number	Size	Type	Description	Value
7013	19"	Phanolith	Trojan warriors on boat, signed Stahl (mate to 7014)	$1700.
7014	19"	Phanolith	Trojan lady and her servants, signed Stahl (mate to 7013)	$1700.
7025	15½"x12"	Phanolith	Rectangular, scene from Lohengrin opera, signed Stahl (mate to 7026)	$1600.
7026	15½"x12"	Phanolith	Rectangular, scene from Lohengrin opera, signed Stahl (mate to 7025)	$1600.

7030

Number	Size	Type	Description	Value
7030	24''x11½''	Phanolith	Rectangular, scene from Trojan War, signed Stahl (mate to 7031)	$2400.
7031	24''x11½''	Phanolith	Rectangular, scene from Trojan War, signed Stahl (mate to 7030)	$2400.
7032	9''	Phanolith	Oval shaped, woman's profile (mate to 7033)	$250.
7033	9''	Phanolith	Oval shaped, woman's profile (mate to 7032)	$250.
7036	18''	Phanolith	Harvesting scene (mate to 7037)	$1100.
7037	18''	Phanolith	Dancing scene (mate to 7036)	$1100.

7032, 7033

7036, 7037

Number	Size	Type	Description	Value
7040	21''	Phanolith	Three mythological figures, signed Stahl (mate to 7043)	$1400.
7041	15½''x12''	Phanolith	Rectangular, *words of love,* serenade scene (mate to 7042)	$1600.
7042	15½''x12''	Phanolith	Rectangular, *words of love,* serenade scene (matc to 7041)	$1600.

7040, 7043

7045

7053

Number	Size	Type	Description	Value
7043	21"	Phanolith	Three mythological figures and dolphin (mate to 7040)	$1400.
7044	15½"x8"	Phanolith	Rectangular, young man and maiden (mate to 7045)	$1400.
7045	15½"x8"	Phanolith	Rectangular, young man and maiden (mate to 7044)	$1400.
7046	15½"x12"	Phanolith	Rectangular, scene from *Flying Dutchman* (mate to 7047)	$1500.

7051

Number	Size	Type	Description	Value
7047	15½"x12"	Phanolith	Rectangular, scene from *Flying Dutchman* (mate to 7046)	$1500.
7048	14½"	Phanolith	Chess game, three children (mate to 7049, same scene as 7059)	$900.
7049	14½"	Phanolith	Card game, three children (mate to 7048, same scene as 7060)	$900.
7050	24"x11½"	Phanolith	Rectangular, wedding, signed Stahl (mate to 7051)	$2200.
7051	24"x11½"	Phanolith	Rectangular, children playing, signed Stahl (mate to 7050)	$2200.

7054, 7055

Number	Size	Type	Description	Value
7052	21"	Phanolith	Women figures (mate to 7053)	$1400.
7053	21"	Phanolith	Three women dancing (mate to 7052)	$1400.
7054	9"x7½"	Phanolith	Oval shaped, two girls offering gifts to third (mate to 7055)	$350.
7055	9"x7½"	Phanolith	Oval shaped, one girl kissing another girl and being attacked by third (mate to 7054)	$350.

7066, 7067, 7068

Number	Size	Type	Description	Value
7059	15½"x12"	Phanolith	Rectangular, three children, chess game (mate to 7060, same scene as 7048)	$1000.
7060	15½"x12"	Phanolith	Rectangular, three children, card game (mate to 7059, same scene as 7049)	$1000.
7061	15½"x12"	Phanolith	Rectangular, general leaving on horseback (mate to 7062)	$1100.
7062	15½"x12"	Phanolith	Rectangular, general returning on horseback (mate to 7061)	$1100.

7071, 7072

Number	Size	Type	Description	Value
7066	6"x6"	Phanolith	Square, lady holding mirror, signed Stahl	$325.
7067	4"x6"	Phanolith	Rectangular, woman with artist's palette, signed Stahl (mate to 7068)	$300.
7068	4"x6"	Phanolith	Rectangular, sculptor with angel and statue, signed Stahl (mate to 7067)	$300.
7069	2½"x4"	Phanolith	Oval shaped, woman wrapped in long sash (mate to 7070)	$175.
7069	4"x6"	Phanolith		$300.

7069, 7070

Number	Size	Type	Description	Value
7070	2½"x4"	Phanolith	Oval shaped, woman wearing long sash, holding lyre and flowers (mate to 7069)	$175.
7070	4"x6"	Phanolith		$300.
7071	6"x8"	Phanolith	Rectangular, lady holding jewel box in one hand and jewels in other (mate to 7072)	$325.
7072	6"x8"	Phanolith	Rectangular, lady holding flowers (mate to 7071)	$325.

7073, 7074

Number	Size	Type	Description	Value
7073	8"x8"	Phanolith	Square, Cupid standing on ornate fountain, giving Venus drink, signed Stahl (mate to 7074)	$400.
7074	8"x8"	Phanolith	Square, Cupid standing on ornate fountain, being held by Venus, signed Stahl (mate to 7073)	$400.
		Set of Four		
7075	8"x6"	Phanolith	Rectangular, girl in Spring scene	$350.
7076	8"x6"	Phanolith	Rectangular, girl in Summer scene	$350.
7077	8"x6"	Phanolith	Rectangular, girl in Fall scene	$350.
7078	8"x6"	Phanolith	Rectangular, girl in Winter scene	$350.
7079	8"x6"	Phanolith	Rectangular, man and woman sitting on tree stumps in field with sheep, signed Stahl (mate to 7080)	$350.

Number	Size	Type	Description	Value
7080	8"x6"	Phanolith	Rectangular, girl seated and young man on one knee, sheep and dog in background, signed Stahl (mate to 7079)	$350.
7083	8"x6"	Phanolith	Rectangular, Cupid pouring flowers on woman, signed Stahl	$350.

7075, 7076

7077   7078

Plaques in set 7075 to 7078 are frequently numbered incorrectly.

7079, 7080

6. Beakers

Villeroy & Boch/Mettlach made a few styles of beakers that were not print under glaze. These are listed here first, in the order of their incised form numbers. These non-PUG beakers are mostly of the typical truncated conical shape, with the exception of the Boots (225), Roemers (2953 and 2954) and the Renaissance Lady (5045) which could be subclassified as *character beakers*.

The vast majority of Mettlach beakers are the PUGs that were made on two forms, 2327 and 2368. The listing of the PUG beakers follows the short non-PUG listing and is in order by decoration numbers. Some of the PUG beakers may be found with handles, which slightly increases their value.

Number	Size	Type	Description	Value
225	.75L	Glazed	Boot character beaker	$400.
225	1.0L	Glazed		$475.
1218	.25L	Relief	Six panels, pedestal base	$125.
1328	.25L	Mosaic	Geometric design (with handle)	$100.
1335	.25L	Mosaic	Geometric design (with handle)	$100.

225 .75L

1218

2389

2781, 2815

2834

Number	Size	Type	Description	Value
1350	.25L	Mosaic	Geometric design	$100.
1380	.25L	Glazed	Plain (with handle)	$70.
1381	.25L	Glazed	Plain (with handle)	$70.
1420	.25L	Mosaic	Geometric design	$120.
2360	.25L	Relief	Cherubs hunting	$125.
2389	.25L	Relief	Cherubs	$125.
2390	.25L	Relief	Peasants	$125.
2439	.25L	Relief	Simple design, glazed	$70.
Set of Three				
2781	.25L	Cameo	Lovers	$300.
2815	.25L	Cameo	Dancing	$300.
2816	.25L	Cameo	Dancing	$300.
2834	.25L	Mosaic	Floral decoration	$150.
2897	.25L	Etched	Art nouveau, geometric design	$100.
2904	.25L	Etched	Art nouveau, geometric design	$100.
2953	.25L	Relief	Floral design	$100.
2968	.25L	Glazed	Plain, brown glazed bands	$30.
Set of Three				
3325	.25L	Etched	Cavaliers drinking (matches stein 1932)	$300.
3326	.25L	Etched	Barmaid and drinker (matches stein 2640)	$300.
3327	.25L	Etched	Man playing guitar for lady (matches stein 2780)	$300.

Number	Size	Type	Description	Value
3365	.25L	Etched	Art nouveau design	$120.
5045	.5L	Glazed	Renaissance lady, character beaker or quaffer	$1200.

The following are PUG beakers in order of decoration numbers:

Set of Six

235(2327)	.25L	PUG	Man with guitar	$85.
236(2327)	.25L	PUG	Man drinking	$85.
237(2327)	.25L	PUG	Boy with flute	$85.
238(2327)	.25L	PUG	Tyrolean man (matches stein 238 [1909])	$85.
239(2327)	.25L	PUG	Man and woman (matches stein 239 [1909])	$85.
240(2327)	.25L	PUG	Hunter (matches stein 240[1909])	$85.

Set of Six

425(2327)	.25L	PUG	*Bremen city hall*	$85.
426(2327)	.25L	PUG	*Hamburg*	$85.
427(2327)	.25L	PUG	*Brandenberg Tor*	$85.
428(2327)	.25L	PUG	*Heidelberg castle*	$85.
429(2327)	.25L	PUG	*Nurnberg*	$85.
430(2327)	.25L	PUG	*Hofbrauhaus*	$95.

3325   3326   3327   3365

235, 237, 239, 426, 428, 430

Number	Size	Type	Description	Value
1014(2368)	.25L	PUG	Munich Child (matches steins 2767 and 1014[2262], plaque 1044/1014)	$80.

Set of Three

Number	Size	Type	Description	Value
1023(2327)	.25L	PUG	Fiddler (master is stein 1022[2348], matches stein 1023[2349])	$50.
1024(2327)	.25L	PUG	Flute player (master is 1022[2348], matches stein 1024[2349])	$50.
1025(2327)	.25L	PUG	Barmaid (master is stein 1022[2348], matches stein 1025 [2349])	$50.
1029(2327)	.25L	PUG	Tavern scene, with various restaurant advertisements	$90.
1032(2368)	.25L	PUG	Gnomes drinking (mate to 1033, master steins are 953[2183] and 1031[2332], matches stein 1032 [2333])	$75.
1033(2368)	.25L	PUG	Gnomes drinking (mate to 1032, master steins are 953[2183] and 1031[2332], matches stein 1033 [2333])	$75.

Number	Size	Type	Description	Value
		Set of Three		
1050(2327)	.25L	PUG	Girl with large jug	$85.
1051(2327)	.25L	PUG	Girl with pitcher, signed CK	$85.
1052(2327)	.25L	PUG	Girl with tray	$85.
		Set of Six		
1091(2368)	.25L	PUG	Waiter serving wine	$70.
1092(2368)	.25L	PUG	Cavalier holding glass	$70.
1093(2368)	.25L	PUG	Cavalier playing mandolin	$70.
1094(2368)	.25L	PUG	Cavalier drinking from stein	$70.
1095(2368)	.25L	PUG	Cavalier smoking pipe and drinking	$70.
1096(2368)	.25L	PUG	Cavalier pouring wine (this set matches plaques 2621 to 2626 and coasters 2817 to 2822)	$70.

1014, 1029, 1032, 1033

1023, 1024, 1025, 1050, 1051, 1052

1091, 1092, 1093, 1094, 1095, 1096

Number	Size	Type	Description	Value
1109(2368)	.25L	PUG	Musicians, signed Schlitt (mate to 1110, matches stein 1109 [1909])	$70.
1110(2368)	.25L	PUG	Soldiers drinking, signed Schlitt (mate to 1109, matches stein 1110[1909])	$75.
		Set of Four		
1134(2327)	.25L	PUG	Man and woman	$85.
1135(2327)	.25L	PUG	Man and woman	$85.
1136(2327)	.25L	PUG	Man and woman	$85.
1137(2327)	.25L	PUG	Man and woman	$85.
		Set of Three		
1139(2368)	.25L	PUG	Violin player	$85.
1140(2368)	.25L	PUG	Three men at table	$85.
1141(2368)	.25L	PUG	Man at table and waitress	$85.

1109, 1110, 1139, 1140, 1141

1170, 1171, 1172, 1173, 1174, 1175

Number	Size	Type	Description	Value
		Set of Six		
1170(2842)	.25L	PUG	Gnome with grapes	$90.
1171(2842)	.25L	PUG	Gnome in tree	$90.
1172(2842)	.25L	PUG	Gnome drinking	$90.
1173(2842)	.25L	PUG	Gnome drinking	$90.
1174(2842)	.25L	PUG	Gnome drinking	$90.
1175(2842)	.25L	PUG	Gnome smoking	$90.
1170 to 1175(2327)	.25L	PUG	Same decorations with different body	$80. each
		Set of Six		
1176(2327)	.25L	PUG	*Games* (matches stein 1176[1909])	$85.
1177(2327)	.25L	PUG	*Music* (matches stein 1177[1909])	$85.
1178(2327)	.25L	PUG	*Beer* (matches stein 1178[1909])	$85.
1179(2327)	.25L	PUG	*Song* (matches stein 1179[1909])	$85.
1180(2327)	.25L	PUG	*Dance* (matches stein 1180[1909])	$85.
1181(2327)	.25L	PUG	*Love* (matches stein 1181[1909])	$85.

1176, 1177, 1178, 1179, 1180, 1181

Number	Size	Type	Description	Value
		Set of Six		
1187(2327)	.25L	PUG	Woman on beach	$50.
1188(2327)	.25L	PUG	Woman on beach	$50.
1189(2327)	.25L	PUG	Woman on beach	$50.
1190(2327)	.25L	PUG	Fisherman smoking	$50.
1191(2327)	.25L	PUG	Fisherman on boat	$50.
1192(2327)	.25L	PUG	Fisherman on beach (master stein to this set is 1197[2893])	$50.
1194(2954)	.25L	PUG	Cupids	$100.
		Set of Twelve		
1200(2327)	.25L	PUG	Twelve different German cities: Berlin, Bremen, Breslau, Dresden, Frankfurt a.M., Hamburg, Hannover, Koln, Leipzig, Munchen, Nurnberg, Stuttgart (master stein for this set is 1200[2893])	$50. each
1200(2327)	.25L	PUG	Same set except with handles	$75. each
1200(2327)	.25L	PUG	Beakers for other German cities	$85. each
1200(2327)	.25L	PUG	*Chicago*	$150.
1200(2327)	.25L	PUG	*Indiana*	$150.
1200(2327)	.25L	PUG	*Cincinnati*	$135.
1200(2327)	.25L	PUG	*St. Louis*	$135.
1200(2327)	.25L	PUG	*Asheville* (North Carolina)	$125.

1200 United States' Cities and States

1200 Series German Cities

Number	Size	Type	Description	Value
1200(2327)	.25L	PUG	*Kansas City*	$150.
1200(2327)	.25L	PUG	*Milwaukee*	$150.
1200(2327)	.25L	PUG	*Seattle*	$135.
1200(2327)	.25L	PUG	*Denver*	$135.
1200(2327)	.25L	PUG	*Moctezuma-Orizaba*	$125.
1200(2327)	.25L	PUG	*Montreal*	$125.
1200(2327)	.25L	PUG	*Toronto*	$125.
1200(2327)	.25L	PUG	*Vancouver*	$125.
1200(2327)	.25L	PUG	*University of Pennsylvania*	$125.
1200(2327)	.25L	PUG	*Columbia University*	$125.
1200(2327)	.25L	PUG	*Yale University*	$125.
1200(2327)	.25L	PUG	*Princeton University*	$125.

Set of Three

1213(2327)	.25L	PUG	Woman holding glass (with handle)	$85.
1214(2327)	.25L	PUG	Woman smoking (with handle)	$85.
1215(2327)	.25L	PUG	Woman with basket of fruit (with handle)	$85.

1194

1213, 1214, 1215

Number	Size	Type	Description	Value
		Set of Six		
1230(2327)	.25L	PUG	Young girl and duck	$100.
1231(2327)	.25L	PUG	Young girl and cat	$100.
1232(2327)	.25L	PUG	Boy sitting on barrel	$100.
1233(2327)	.25L	PUG	Boy and dog	$100.
1234(2327)	.25L	PUG	Boy riding stick horse	$100.
1235(2327)	.25L	PUG	Young girl with tennis racket	$100.
1287(2327)	.25L	PUG	Animals dressed for dinner	$100.

1230, 1231, 1232, 1233, 1234, 1235

Number	Size	Type	Description	Value
		Set of Six		
1290A(2327)	.25L	PUG	State crest of Prussia (matches stein 1290A [2893])	$85.
1290B(2327)	.25L	PUG	State crest of Wurttemberg (matches stein 1290B[2893])	$80.

Number	Size	Type	Description	Value
1290C(2327)	.25L	PUG	State crest of Bavaria (matches stein 1290C[2893])	$80.
1290D(2327)	.25L	PUG	State crest of Saxony (matches stein 1290D [2893])	$80.
1290E(2327)	.25L	PUG	State crest of Hesse (matches stein 1290E [2893])	$80.
1290F(2327)	.25L	PUG	State crest of Baden (matches stein 1290F [2893])	$80.

1290A, 1290B, 1290C, 1290D, 1290E, 1290F

Number	Size	Type	Description	Value
1290H(2327)	.25L	PUG	Coat of arms: Sweden	$100.
1290K(2327)	.25L	PUG	Coat of arms: France	$100.
1302(2327)	.25L	PUG	American eagle (matches stein 1302 [2893])	$150.

1287, 1200 *Univ. Penn.*

1290H, 1290K, 1302

1329, 1330, 1334, 1392

Number	Size	Type	Description	Value
1329(2327)	.25L	PUG	Little Red Riding Hood	$120.
1330(2327)	.25L	PUG	Three girls feeding geese	$120.
1334(2327)	.25L	PUG	Three children with lamb	$120.
1350(2327)	.25L	PUG	*Kaiser Wilhelm* (mate to 1351)	$100.
1351(2327)	.25L	PUG	*Kaiserin* (mate to 1350)	$100.
1392(2327)	.25L	PUG	Hansel and Gretel	$120.
1415(2327)	.25L	PUG	Cat in cape	$120.
1419(2327)	.25L	PUG	Cinderella sitting by fireplace	$100.
1501(2327)	.25L	PUG	Child soldier	$100.

Set of Three

4241(2368)	.25L	PUG	St. Augustine, Florida	$75.
4242(2368)	.25L	PUG	Palm Beach, Florida	$75.
4243(2368)	.25L	PUG	Nassau, Bahamas	$100.

1350, 1351, 1415, 1419, 1501

4241, 4242, 4243, Elk's Club, *Hires Root Beer*

Number	Size	Type	Description	Value
		Set of Three		
6137(2327)	.25L	Rookwood	Cavalier with pipe and stein (matches stein 2792/6137)	$200.
6142(2327)	.25L	Rookwood	Cavalier with pipe and stein (matches stein 2788/6142)	$200.
6146(2327)	.25L	Rookwood	Man drinking (matches stein 2790/6146)	$200.

The following are PUG beakers without decoration numbers:

(2327)	.25L	PUG	*Cape Beer*, Gambrinus straddling barrel	$135.
(2327)	.25L	PUG	*Boston*	$150.
(2327)	.25L	PUG	Elk's Club (matches steins [1526] and [2893])	$50.
(2327)	.25L	PUG	*Hires Root Beer*, beaker with handle	$100.

Banff National Park, *Old Vienna*

11 Deutsches Turnfest, Fraternal crest, Cavalier holding staff

Number	Size	Type	Description	Value
(2327)	.25L	PUG	Fraternal crest	$75.
(2327)	.25L	PUG	*Old Vienna,* Atlantic City	$100.
(2327)	.25L	PUG	*Banff* National Park, Canada, buffalo	$95.
(2327)	.25L	PUG	Cavalier holding staff, 25th wedding anniversary 1875-1900	$95.
(2327)	.25L	PUG	*Salem, Mass.,* witch on broomstick	$150.
(2327)	.25L	PUG	*11 Deutsches Turnfest, 4F, zu Frankfurt am Main 1908*	$150.
(2327)	.25L	PUG	*Taft Brewery,* wine cellar scene	$125.
(3081)	.25L	Bavaria	Grey bodies with geometric or floral designs, decoration numbers can include 401, 402 and 403	$40.

5045

6146

7. Punch Bowls

Mettlach made a small number of what they called *Bowle,* which is a German word for *bowl* that does not suggest any specific use. These bowls, however, have come to be called *punch bowls*, although many were probably also intended for use as soup tureens. Some of the earliest V&B products were mostly functional, everyday wares, including some rather plain items that were definitely for soup. The later Mettlach bowls often are decorated with grape-leaf designs and other festive decorations making them definitely intended for holding beverages. The Mettlach bowls always came with lids, occasionally included plates, and rarely had ceramic ladles.

Number	Size	Type	Description	Value
301	10.0L	Relief	Barrel shape, leaves and vines all over, no plate, young child on top	$550.
375	10.0L	Relief	Animal heads protrude from sides, cow on lid	$650.
418	9.0L	Relief	Scroll and floral decoration, figures form handles	$475.
820	8.0L	Relief	Hunting scene	$500.
1158	16.0L	Relief	Barrel with leaves and vines, no plate, lid is bearded man on throne	$800.
1295	6.3L	Mosaic	Geometric design	$500.
1393	8.0L	Mosaic	Floral design, could have matching ladle	$600.
1859	9.0L	Etched	Tavern scene, signed Warth	$1350.

375

1888b

Number	Size	Type	Description	Value
1880	8.0L	Mosaic	Geometric design	$400.
1888	6.0L	Relief	Prussian eagle, two versions: (a) brown and tan (b) black, gold, tan, crown on lid, no plate	$1200. $1500.

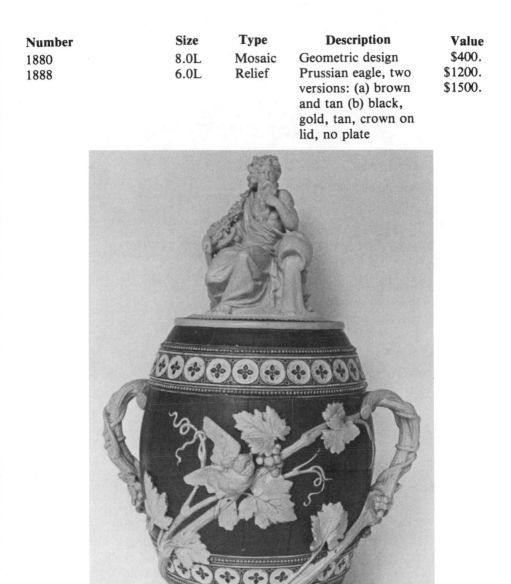

1158

1859

Number	Size	Type	Description	Value
1969	6.0L	Mosaic	Geometric design	$450.
1978	4.0L	Relief	Faces in relief, no plate	$400.
2000	5.0L	Relief	Floral decoration	$450.
2014	5.5L	Etched	St. Hubert bowl, art nouveau design with rabbits and skulls (matches steins 2812 and 2813)	$900.
2087	8.0L	Relief	Dancing scene (matches steins 2085 and 2086)	$400.
2088	8.85L	Etched	Man and woman drinking, cupid overhead, plate has gnome scene, signed Schlitt	$1500.

Number	Size	Type	Description	Value
2119	6.0L	Mosaic	Geometric design	$350.
2129	6.0L	Mosaic	Geometric design	$350.
2225	4.0L	Relief	Barrel shape, leaf and vine decoration, no plate, signed Hein	$200.
2226/989	1.85L	PUG	Gnomes dancing after harvesting grapes, no plate, drunken gnome on lid	$300.
2226/1062	1.85L	PUG	Tavern scene, no plate, drunken gnome on lid (matches steins 955[2180] and 955 [2271])	$300.

2088

Number	Size	Type	Description	Value
2234	6.0L	Relief	Leaves on vines, dwarf on lid	$450.
2280/1005	2.15L	PUG	Gnomes working at wine press and drinking, no plate (matches steins 1009 [1909] and 1010[1909])	$250.
2339/1028	7.5L	PUG	Gnomes working at wine press and drinking (matches steins 1009[1909] and 1010[1909])	$550.
2339/1193	7.5L	PUG	Six scenes of gnomes (matches set of coasters 1032)	$550.
2341	10.0L	Relief	Drunken man, figural handle	$550.

2234

2341

2814

2843

Number	Size	Type	Description	Value
2595/1072	2.0L	PUG	Children eating and drinking, no plate (matches steins 1084 [2177] and 1085[2177])	$250.
2602	5.75L	Cameo	Figures in two panels	$1000.
2633/1089	7.4L	PUG	Dancing scene	$550.
2633/1121	5.7L	PUG	Soldiers drinking	$550.
2694	6.0L	Etched	Flying angels	$1400.
2703/1127	5.4L	PUG	Angels in clouds	$600.
2703/1130	5.4L	PUG	Tavern scene	$475.
2703/1150	5.4L	PUG	Tavern scene	$450.
2806	9.4L	Cameo & Mosaic	Bacchus, two panels	$1000.
2814	7.6L	Etched	Art nouveau, women's portraits	$1500.

Number	Size	Type	Description	Value
2843	8.75L	Etched	Dancing and music scenes, signed Schlitt	$1400.
2890	9.4L	Cameo	Tavern scene	$1000.
2918	6.5L	Etched	Art nouveau, grapes	$650.
2969	8.5L	Cameo	Dancing and music	$1100.
2974	4.5L	Etched	Art nouveau, grapes	$350.
2992	7.0L	Etched	Art nouveau, geometric design	$400.
3037/1209	9.0L	PUG	Six panels, women in each	$450.
3088	6.0L	Etched	Noah and ark, signed Schlitt	$1800.
3149	5.0L	Cameo	Musicians	$1000.
3515	7.0L	Cameo	Wedding scenes, signed Stahl	$900.

2890

3088

3515

8. Pokals

Pokals, or in English called bumpers or brimming cups, are ceremonial drinking vessels which are a carry-over from the elegance and pageantry of earlier eras. Brimmers, which is another appropriate name, consisted of unusually large handleless beakers with pedestal bases and ornate covers. Historically, many beautiful pokals were made of enamelled glass or silver, but the Mettlach versions were naturally of stoneware and shared the same body decorations as some of the larger steins.

Only a small number of pokals were made by Mettlach and they all came with lids. These lids have occasionally been lost or discarded with the bases inappropriately sold as vases.

Number	Size	Type	Description	Value
168	1.1L	Relief	Drinking scenes, spirals upward around body	$475.
208	1.5L	Relief	Leaves, platinum accenting	$150.
231	1.5L	Relief	Building the Cologne Cathedral	$400.
396	1.3L	Relief	Four panels of figures	$500.
454	1.4L	Relief	Gambrinus drinking	$350.
454	2.25L	Relief		$400.
734	2.1L	Relief	Six panels	$450.
1004	2.7L	Relief	Four panels of figures, boy on barrel on lid	$550.
1247	2.6L	Relief	Busts of Nurnberg artists (matches stein 1169)	$500.

208, 231, 454 1.4L

Number	Size	Type	Description	Value
1735	2.2L	Etched	Lovers, signed Warth (matches stein 1734)	$900.
1785	1.75L	Etched	Four panels, troubadour and knights, signed Warth (matches stein 2003)	$900.
1820	1.8L	Etched & Relief	Four panels of figures, full color relief (matches stein 1809)	$800.
1971	2.0L	Mosaic	Floral design	$350.
2058	3.0L	Etched & Relief	Monkeys at play, monkey on lid	$1800.
2063	3.25L	Etched	St. Hubert and stag, fox on lid	$2000.
2066	2.5L	Etched	Man and barmaid, signed Schlitt (matches stein 2065)	$900.

Number	Size	Type	Description	Value
2084	3.5L	Etched	Shooting match scenes, four panels, boy on lid	$2000.
2110	2.5L	Etched	Gambrinus on throne, signed Schlitt (matches stein 2107)	$1000.

1735, 2066, 2110

Number	Size	Type	Description	Value
2132	.95L	Relief	Man drinking (matches stein 2130)	$375.
2150	1.6L	Relief	Figural scene wraps around body, castle on lid	$650.
2385	5.0L	Relief	Three panels of figures, three handles	$650.
2418	2.3L	Relief	Woman dancing, tall pedestal base, boy on lid	$700.

168, 2132, 2523

2058

1785

Number	Size	Type	Description	Value
2522	1.2L	Cameo	Athletic scenes, signed Stahl	$950.
2523	1.2L	Cameo	Singing scenes, signed Stahl	$950.

2063

2084

9. Vases

As with the pokals, some of the Mettlach vases shared the same decorations as steins. There were, however, a great many vases that carried unique designs, and in this respect they seem to have been less an afterthought and more popular than the pokals.

Mettlach produced over 200 different vases, including cameo, etched, relief, mosaic, Delft, and Rookwood styles in a tremendous range of sizes. The following are some examples of these vases.

Number	Size	Type	Description	Value
—	9"	Relief	Tree trunk style, two handles, leaves and acorns, platinum accenting	$125.
28	7"	Relief	Dancing figures, two panels	$100.
28	7½"	Relief		$125.
327	12½"	Relief	Leaves, children form handles	$140.
1241	13½"	Relief	Geometric design	$150.
1289	11"	Mosaic	Geometric design	$175.
1354	29"	Etched	Woman and child (mate to 1491)	$2000.
1383	10"	Etched	Birds	$250.
1462	13"	Etched	Four panels, women	$250.
1464	2½"	Mosaic	Geometric design	$70.
1491	29"	Etched	Woman and child (mate to 1354)	$2000.

Tree Trunk Vase 9"   28   7"   327

Number	Size	Type	Description	Value
1537	14½"	Etched	Four panels, children	$350.
1538	30"	Relief	Birds and flowers, full color relief	$1200.
1567	22"	Relief	Birds, full color relief	$1000.
1728	6"	Mosiac	Geometric design	$125.

1241, 1462, 1537

Number	Size	Type	Description	Value
1749	13"	Etched	Woman with flowers	$300.
1779	6"	Mosaic	Geometric design	$125.
1829	9½"	Relief	Geometric design, full color relief	$125.
1875	9"	Mosaic	Geometric design	$125.
1884	13"	Mosaic	Geometric design	$175.

1749, 1829

Number	Size	Type	Description	Value
2017	13"	Mosaic	Geometric design, gargoyle spout	$300.
2127	13"	Etched	Children	$375.
2174	6½"	Etched	Woman's portrait	$175.
2207	16½"	Etched	Lovers	$500.
2209	17"	Etched	Siegfried scenes	$1000.
2239	15"	Etched	Children playing	$300.
2242	14"	Etched	Woman seated	$275.
2253	12½"	Etched	Cavalier and lady dancing	$375.
2254	14"	Etched	Children playing	$400.
2279	13"	Etched	Wedding scene	$350.
2301	15½"	Etched	Children	$450.
2301	27"	Etched		$600.
2328	13½"	Etched	Woman and cherub	$300.

2209

2242, 2253, 2279

1567

Number	Size	Type	Description	Value
2414	13½"	Etched	Art nouveau, flowers	$225.
2414	17"	Etched		$275.
2416	16"	Etched	Art nouveau, flowers	$700.
2420	13½"	Etched	Art nouveau, flowers	$400.
2422	13"	Etched	Art nouveau, flowers	$325.
2424	10"	Etched	Art nouveau, girl's portrait (mate to 2425)	$550.
2425	10"	Etched	Art nouveau, girl's portrait (mate to 2424)	$550.
2431	12"	Cameo	Children playing, signed Stahl	$300.
2432	10"	Cameo	Children playing	$200.
2446	14"	Cameo	Roman scene	$350.
2447	11"	Cameo	Mythological figures	$350.

2451, 2431

2414 17'', 2420

Number	Size	Type	Description	Value
2451	10''	Cameo	Mythological figures	$250.
2453	16''	Etched	Woman dancing	$375.
2467	12''	Etched	Art nouveau, flowers	$400.
2483	13''	Etched	Little Red Riding Hood	$500.
2537	13''	Etched	Flowers	$275.
2704/6108	16''	Rookwood	Man's portrait	$500.
2704/6109	16''	Rookwood	Woman's portrait	$500.
2909	17''	Etched	Art nouveau, flowers	$500.

2909   2416

10. Other Wares

In the humble beginnings of the predecessors to Villeroy & Boch there was a concentration on tablewares and useful household items. Many of these products continued to be made somewhat into the real beginning of the "stein era" in the 1880's. It must have been elegant indeed to have a table set with serving pieces that matched the decorations on the master pitcher and steins. There was something of a revival of the production of the miscellaneous items when the art nouveau designs became popular after the turn of the century. The following is a small sampling of these items and their current values.

Number	Size	Type	Description	Value
		Ash Trays		
2883	6" diameter	Etched	Art nouveau, floral design	$150.
2963	6" diameter	Etched	Art nouveau, girl's portrait	$250.
		Beer Taps		
2649	19" height	Etched	*Die Kannenburg,* knight in castle, signed Schlitt (matches steins 2524 and 2580)	$3000.
2666	34" height	Hand Painted	Deer, with matching lid	$1000.
2684	19" height	Etched	*Die Kannenburg,* Knight in castle, signed Schlitt (matches steins 2524 and 2580)	$3000.

2666 Beer Tap

2649 Beer Tap

464 Cigar Holder

Number	Size	Type	Description	Value
		Butter Dish		
1312	3" height	Mosaic	Geometric design	$125.
		Cigar Holder		
464	7" height	Relief	Tree trunk style, gnome	$250.
		Clocks		
2487	16" height	Etched	Angel, sleeping man, rooster, and owl, Etruscan style	$2500.
7034	10" height	Phanolith	Mythological figures	$1500.
		Coasters		
1032	4¾" diameter	PUG	Set of six different scenes of gnomes (matches stein 953 [2183] and bowl 2339/1193	$75. each
2817 to 2822	4½" diameter	Etched	Set of six different scenes (matches plaques 2621 to 2626 and beakers 1091 to 1096[2368])	$150. each

Number	Size	Type	Description	Value
		Figurines		
2153	10" height		Young man, full color	$650.
2157	11" height		Man with beer barrel and glass, full color	$800.
2158	10½" height		Man drinking, full color	$800.
		Flower Pots		
1128	16" height	Etched	Mettlach town scenes, figural handles	$2500.
1355	23" height	Etched	Garden scene, cupids seated on handles	$4500.
1360	15½" height	Mosaic	Floral design	$400.
2417	8" height	Etched	Art nouveau, flowers	$650.

1355 Flower Pot

Number	Size	Type	Description	Value
		Honey Jars		
1198	3½'' height	Mosaic	Geometric design	$100.
1324	4½'' height	Mosaic	Floral design	$125.
		Inkwell		
121	6'' height	Relief	Leaves, cherub on lid	$225.
		Lampbases		
1236	9'' height	Mosaic	Geometric design	$275.
1358	9'' height	Mosaic	Floral design	$350.
		Liquor Set		
1328	8'' height	Mosaic	Geometric design, bottle and six beakers with tray	$850.

7012, 7024 Pitchers

121 Inkwell

2167 Loving Cup

Number	Size	Type	Description	Value
		Loving Cup		
2167	6'' height	Etched	*Bacchus* carousing, three handles (matches stein 2035)	$300.
		Pitchers		
7012	12'' height	Phanolith	Dancing	$800.
7022	16'' height	Phanolith	Musicians and dancing	$1000.
7023	17'' height	Phanolith	Mythological figures	$1600.
7024	15'' height	Phanolith	Flowers and leaves	$950.

Number	Size	Type	Description	Value
		Salad Bowls		
1308	5" height	Mosaic	Floral design	$175.
1309	4" height	Mosaic	Floral design	$150.
1321	4½" height	Mosaic	Geometric design	$175.

7023 Pitcher

Number	Size	Type	Description	Value
		Tobacco Jars		
116	7" height	Relief	Six panels, figures in each	$150.
337	8" height	Relief	Tree trunk style, figure of man in front also match holder and strike, boy on lid	$450.
1231	7" height	Etched	Cattle	$300.
1305	6½" height	Mosaic	Geometric design	$200.
2881	8½" height	Etched	Art nouveau design	$300.

116 Tobacco Jar

337 Tobacco Jar

2881 Tobacco Jar

11. Bibliography and References

Clarke, P.J., and J. O'Connor, 1977. "The Mettlach Occupationalists," *Prosit, 48,* Stein Collectors International, p. 408, June.

Cohausen, A. von, 1879. "Einige technische Bemerkungen uber die groberen Thonwaaren auf der Pariser Austellung 1878," in *Mittheilungen des Gewerbevereins fur Nassau.*

DeSelms, R.C., 1978. "Oh, Your Ritter's Mustache," *Prosit, 54,* Stein Collectors International, p. 521, December.

Erben, W., 1913. "Dombecher," in *Alt-Koln, 5,* p. 71.

Fox, R., 1979. "Probe," *Prosit, 58,* Stein Collectors International, p. 627-628, December.

Gruhl, J., 1982. "Queen of the Drinking Vessels," *Prosit, 70,* Stein Collectors International, p.978-980, December.

Gruner, E., 1968. *Geschichte der Familie Boch,* Saarbrucken.

Hansen, H.J., 1970. *Das pompose Zeitalter zwischen Biedermeier und Jugendstil,* Gerhard Stallung Verlag, Oldenburg.

Harrell, J.L., 1979. *Regimental Steins,* The Old Soldier Press, Frederick, Maryland.

Hillier, B., 1968. *Pottery and Porcelain 1700-1914, The Social History of Decorative Arts,* London.

Hirschfeld, P., 1885. "Die Firma Villeroy & Boch auf der 1885er Weltausstellung von Antwerpen," in *Export,* Report of the Central-Vereins fur Handelsgeographie zu Berlin.

Hoch, A.A., 1975. "Breaking the German Code," *Prosit, 41,* Stein Collectors International, p. 281, September.

Honeker, H., 1965. "Mettlacher Steins in den USA," in *Keramos, 4,* research newspaper Villeroy & Boch, p. 18-19.

Kirsner, G., 1982. "Signatures on Etched Mettlach Steins: What are They Worth?," *Stein Report,* June.

1 'Encyclopedie Contemporaine, 1900. "Les porcelaines et cristux des fabriques Villeroy & Boch de Mettlach an der Saar," University Sciences, Arts, Industries, Paris, *439,* p. 99, July 31.

Lowenstein, J.G., 1974. *A Stein Bibliography,* Princeton NJ.

Lowenstein, J.G., 1976. "The V and B Chromolith Technique - One Theory," *Prosit, 46,* Stein Collectors International, p. 365.

Lowenstein, J.G., and P. Clarke, 1974. *English Translation 1899 Mettlach Catalogue with Supplement Steins,* Princeton NJ.

Ortzen, P. von, 1965. "Eine interessante Begegnung (Commes, Speicher)," in *Keramos, 4,* research newspaper Villeroy & Boch, p. 9-10.

Ratius, G., 1969. "Die Mettlach Steins haben es ihnen angetan," in *Keramos, 4,* research newspaper Villeroy & Boch, p. 16-18.

Thieler, E.R., 1909. *Making Steins in an Old Monastery,* Brochure by E.R. Thieler Co.

Thomas, T., 1971. "Role des Boch Dans la Ceramique des 18e et 19e Siecles," Institut Superieur D'Histoire de L'art et d'Archeologie, University of Leige.

Thomas, T., 1973. "225 Jahre Boch'sche Keramik," in *Keramos, 5,* research newspaper Villeroy & Boch, p. 10-17.

Thomas, T., 1974. *Die Rolle der beiden Familien Boch & Villeroy im 18. and 19. Jahrhundert: Die Entstehung des Unternehmens Villeroy & Boch,* Saarbrucken.

Thomas, T., 1975. "Jugendstil - auch bei Villeroy & Boch," in *Keramos,* research newspaper Villeroy & Boch, p. 11-14.

Thomas, T., 1976. "Mettlacher Steinzeug - Spiegel des Zeitgeschmacks," in *Keramos,* research newspaper Villeroy & Boch, p. 28-30.

Thomas, T., (ed.), 1978. *Keramos, 6,* Augsburger Druck- und Verlagshaus, Augsburg.

Thomas, T., and A. Post, 1975. *Mettlacher Steinzeug 1885 - 1905,* Ammelounx, Hans J., Publisher, Wheeling, IL.

Wilson, R.D., 1979. "Date Your Mettlach Steins," *Prosit, 57,* Stein Collectors International, p. 597-598, September.

Wilson, R.D., 1979. "Mettlach Mercury Mark Date Code," *Stein Zeitung,* S.C.I. Erste Gruppe, Autumn.

Wilson, R.D., 1980. "Mettlach's Phanolith Fabrication," *Stein Zeitung,* S.C.I. Erste Gruppe, Spring.

Wilson, R.D., 1980. "Mettlach Form Inspector No. and Molder Identification," *Stein Talk, 37,* S.C.I. Thirsty Knights Chapter, June.

Wilson, R.D., 1980. "Mettlach Size Number Code," *Stein Talk, 39,* S.C.I. Thirsty Knights Chapter, December.

Wilson, R.D., 1981. "Changes in Mettlach Marking in 1899," *Stein Zeitung,* S.C.I. Erste Gruppe, September.

Wilson, R.D., 1982. "Misconceptions About Dates Implied By *Made in Germany* on Steins," *Stein Zeitung,* S.C.I. Erste Gruppe, Summer.

Wolff, A., 1970. "Der Mettlacher Dombecher von 1845 und seine Nachfolger," in *Kolner Domblatt, 31-32,* p. 29-52.

Zobeltitz, H. von, 1899. "Villeroy & Boch," in *Velhagen und Klassing's Monatesheften XIII,* Bd. 1, p. 193-207.

Catalogs

Amsterdam, 1977. *Villeroy & Boch 1748 - 1930, Two Centuries of Ceramic Products,* Rijksmuseum Amsterdam.

Bonn, 1976. *Villeroy & Boch - Keramik vom Barock bis zur Neuen Sachlichkeit,* Landesvertretung des Saarlandes, Bonn.

Frankfurt, Munich, and Berlin, 1974. *Aspekte der Grunderzeit,* Frankfurter Kunstverein, Munchner Stadtmuseum, and Akademie der Kunste Berlin.

Mettlach, 1937. *Dreitausend Jahre Topferkunst: Ein Rundgang durch das Keramische Museum von Villeroy & Boch.*

Munich, 1976. *Villeroy & Boch - Keramik vom Barock bis zur Neuen Sachlichkeit,* Munchner Stadtmuseum.

Munich, 1976. *125 Jahre Bayerischer Kunstgewerbeverein,* Munchner Stadt-museum.

Oshkosh, 1969. *Antique Steins at the Paine Art Center.*

Thieler, E.R., 1909. *Mettlach Wares Catalog.*

Journals

Der Gemutlichkeit, Stein Collectors International, *1,* September 1965, to *16,* June 1969.

Keramos, Villeroy & Boch Keramische Werke K.G., *1,* 1952, to *6,* 1978.

Mettlacher Turm, Mettlacher Steinzeugsammler E.V., *1,* 1977, to *10,* 1981.

Prosit, Stein Collectors International, *17,* September 1969, to *70,* December 1982.

Appendix A. Price Adjustments for Condition and Variations

Essential considerations in determining the value of a particular Mettlach item are its quality and condition. That is to say, how well was this stein, plaque, or whatever, originally made as compared to other examples of the same item; and how well has this piece been treated over the years, has it been damaged or abused?

When a stein is examined to determined the original manufacturing quality, it is important to keep in mind that Mettlach steins are very rarely found in absolutely flawless condition, at least not in terms of an uncirculated or proof coin. There were manufacturing variations in the quality (depth and completeness) of the etching, in the coloring, and in the care with which the glaze was applied. Firing lines frequently occurred, as well as air-pocket bubbles, flat spots, or ridges. The presence or lack of any of these factors may or may not have an influence on the value of the particular item, as will be discussed in this appendix.

A.1 Etching

The depth of the etching (incisions) has an important influence on the overall appearance of a stein; when the etching is strong (deep) it generally looks better than when it is weak (shallow). The greatest variation in the quality of the etching usually occurs on steins with form numbers lower than 2000. Steins numbered from 2000 to 2600 tend to be fairly consistent, with only a low percentage having weak etching. Steins numbered above 2600 are quite consistently found with strong etching. When a stein has unusually weak (Fig. 30) or strong (Fig. 31) etching it can influence the price by about 5 to 10%.

<table>
<tr><td>Fig. 30 Detail of 1795
.5L with weak etching</td><td>Fig. 31 Detail of 1795
.5L with strong etching</td></tr>
</table>

A.2 Coloring

Although variations in background colors on the relief steins are sometimes common, major color variations on etched or mosaic steins are fairly rare. The gray or bright green *Prosit* sign on the 2100, or the brown or light blue background color on the 1527, are notable exceptions. Usually when color variations occur it is a light green which is occasionally found instead of dark green, or other subtle differences. For the major color variations the rarer and more attractive versions may carry as much as a 10% premium in value; minor variations will not affect the value.

Blotching or streaking of colors, on the other hand, will definitely affect the value, and depending upon the effect to the appearance of the piece a value adjustment of as much as 10% may be possible. The most common type of blotching seems to occur in the sky portion of scenes. The area of a stein that is most frequently blotched or rough is right inside the handle, due to the technique used in constructing the steins. Imperfections in coloring that are near the handle, however, because they are so common and so unnoticeable, have no influence on the value of the pieces.

A.3 Glaze

Three types of glaze variations deserve some attention in the inspection of a piece of Mettlach ware. First, there are glazes that are counted upon for providing bodies of color or highlights to the scene on a piece; problems with these glazes ought to be treated as described in the previous coloring section. Second, etched designs generally have a dull matte-finish glaze; when an item is found with a light, semi-gloss glaze its appearance will be a little better, and a slight premium, up to 5%, is generally found added to the value. Finally, the bands and handle of steins are usually uniformly glazed with a color. Although some overlap of glazed colors is bound to occur, serious overlaps and sloppy, runny coloring will affect the desirability of a piece. Very sloppy items may carry a 10% reduction in price, but such examples are quite rare.

A.4 Firing Lines

Firing lines or tears in the decorative panel occur on many etched steins. They are lines that appear to be etched lines that are usually less than an inch in length and can change direction three or four times, giving a ragged appearance. Most firing lines are not readily seen, as the design hides them, they are at the bottom of the scene, or back near the handle. Only a very heavy concentration of firing lines (Fig. 32) that are readily visible from a distance, or one or two lines located in a strategic location, such as on a principal character's face, will have an influence on the value of an item. Adjustments of as much as 15% are sometimes necessary before collectors will be willing to accept such visually displeasing flaws.

Fig. 32 Detail of firing lines on 2690 1.4L, note the lines on the legs of the seated man

A.5 Other Factory Flaws

Cameo, mosaic, art nouveau, tapestry, and relief items are subject to the same kinds of manufacturing flaws that often occur in etched pieces, and value adjustments should be made in the same way. Bubbles occurring under the surface of items, when unopened will not affect value, when opened ought to be considered the same as small chips. Flat spots which can be felt but are difficult to see, or low ridges where they were not intended, will have no effect on value.

Print under glaze and faience steins are subject to other types of manufacturing flaws, such as dull coloring, transfer distortions, and glaze browning. The dull coloring, when it occurs, is most noticeable in the reds and blues, and adjustments up to 10% may be required. Streaks, tears, or gaps in the transfer of the decoration must be evaluated in regard to the effect on the visual appeal of the design. Should a great deal of distortion occur an adjustment of as much as 20% could be required. Darkening and blotching of the transfer printed or hand painted wares can have an important effect on the overall appearance of a piece, and adjustments up to 15% are sometimes necessary in order to make a fair valuation.

A.6 Interior Stains

An incomplete interior glazing of a stein, particularly common on inserted ceramic lids, will usually result in a slight brownish stain. The reason for this stain is that, apparently, the stoneware requires the protection of the glaze to withstand the heat of the firing; it is not beer that is causing the stain. Stains can also occur if pens were stored in a stein or beaker with the point down. Interior stains should not affect the value of a stein or vase, unless the surface has reached the point of being pitted or chipped. This occurs quite rarely, and lowers the value by about 10 to 15%.

It ought to be noted that adjustments for factory flaws should not be multiplied or added. That is to say, do not combine two adjustments of 10% to yield 19% or 20%. Instead a deduction of about 15% is usually more realistic. This is also true for multiple adjustments due to damages or improper lids, and so forth.

A.7 Lids

The prices for steins shown in this book are based upon the stein having the specific lid type that is noted in the listing. It should be explained that many steins came with a choice of plain or fancy pewter lids, ceramic insert lids, or no lids. In most cases, however, for etched, cameo, relief, mosaic, and art nouveau steins that are 1 liter or smaller, the most desirable lids generally have the inlaid ceramic inserts. Larger sizes sometimes came only with pewter lids. When a stein is found without a lid, or with a lid (Fig. 33) other than the most desirable type, it will almost always be necessary to lower the value from that which is listed.

Fig. 33 1163 .5L value with pewter lid as shown
$375., 2082 1.0L value with pewter lid as shown
$1300.

The usual situation of this type is for a stein that has an inlaid lid as its most desirable, instead being found with a pewter lid. The extent of the reduction in value will depend upon how appealing the pewter lid is. In some rare cases a stein with a fairly fancy and well-designed pewter lid (Fig. 34) might be worth as much as a stein with the inlay. This is generally true only for ½-liter steins priced under $600, 1-liters under $900, and where the inlay design is not integrally important to the story or the design of the stein. In most cases, it will be necessary to reduce the price between 10% and 35% if the stein has a pewter lid. Should the pewter lid be of a plain dome or flat style with no design, or of an unattractive steeple design, it might be necessary to reduce the price by more than 35%.

Generally speaking, more expensive steins would have to be reduced proportionately more for having pewter lids. In some cases, such as with steins 2765, 2829, or other steins with conical, turret, castle, or other types of fancy inlays, a pewter lid could reduce the value by as much as 45%. Pewter lids were generally not made for such steins with the exception of 1161 and the Football stein 2324.

Lower-priced steins, such as relief steins, are generally worth about the same or just slightly less should they have a pewter lid instead of an inlay lid.

Print under glaze steins come with either fancy pewter lids or plain dome lids. Generally the short PUG steins numbered under 700 have plain lids. No reduction should be necessary for a PUG stein with a plain lid instead of a fancy lid, except in the case of some of the tall ½-liter and 1-liter steins priced over $275. A reduction of 5 to 10% would be sufficient.

Should a stein be missing a lid it is always worth much less than a stein with a lid. Very few steins were originally ordered without lids. Reductions for lidless steins are generally in excess of 50%. The more expensive steins will usually have somewhat lower reductions for missing lids, because here it becomes worthwhile to seek a replacement or a newly constructed lid so as to have a piece for display.

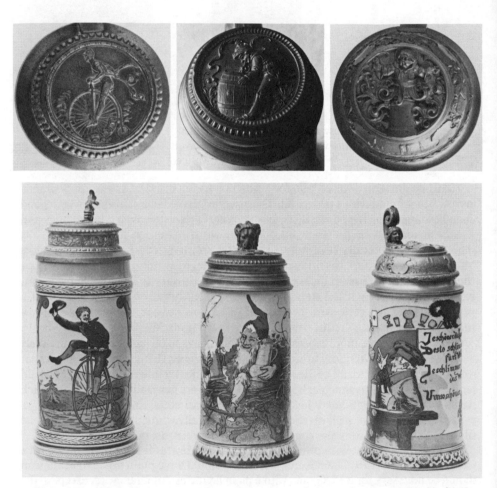

Fig. 34 Three steins with fancy pewter lids, the values as shown, 1566 .5L $850., 2134 .5L $1100., 2090 .5L $550.

A.8 Metal Lids

Lids made from metals other than pewter are occasionally encountered on Mettlach steins. These generally occur on ½-liter steins made before 1900. In the case of sterling or 800-silver lids the value is not significantly reduced where the stein is of low or moderate value and the inlaid lid was not integral to the design. On the other hand, silver-plated, copper, brass, or other metallic lids (Fig. 35) are worth substantially less, reducing values by about 30 to 50%.

Fig. 35 1396 .5L value
with metal lid as shown $300.

A.9 Pewter Damage

Pewter damage occurs frequently on Mettlach steins, but in most cases the damage can be repaired to almost the original condition.

A hinge that will not open can be cleaned with water (do not use oil). If this does not make the hinge operable have an experienced person deal with the problem. A tooth or ring missing from the hinge has only a nominal influence on value, less than 5%.

If a thumblift has been replaced it should result in a reduction of less than 10% from the value of the stein. A missing thumblift will detract about 20%, as will missing finials on ornate all-pewter lids. A tear in the pewter rim reduces the value by 5 to 10%. Dings and dents to the lid will also be in this range unless they are easily reparable.

Properly done repairs to the pewter strap around the handle have only a nominal influence on the value of the stein. However, since strap repairs often mean the lid has been replaced, carefully check to see that this is the appropriate lid for the stein - the colors and design should be in harmony with the body design.

Should a stein that was missing a lid have been provided with a replacement pewter lid, a reduction in value will be necessary. If the pewter lid is of high quality, and is attached properly, a reduction need not be significantly greater than the reduction for a pewter lid where an inlaid lid is normally found, 10 to 35%. Should the lid be an obvious misfit, and poorly attached, the reduction in value should approach that for the stein with no lid, in excess of 50%.

Engraved names on the pewter portion of lids should not reduce the value of a stein unless they have been crudely scratched in. In rare cases the pewter on a stein may be "diseased," having a very dark heavy crust which is sometimes pitted or peeling. When this is encountered a reduction of about 10% in value is necessary, or more if the pewter is eaten through along the bottom.

A.10 Body Damage

Steins and other Mettlach wares are not exceptionally fragile, but over the course of a century damage is likely to occur. With further time, of course, damage will become increasingly common. Damage and repairs can have a significant influence on the value of Mettlach items. Cracks, chips, missing parts, and similar problems will affect the value of items very differently, however there are some general rules that can be followed. A list is presented here of the approximate reductions in value that occur for various types of repaired damage.

Repaired Damage	Value Reduction
Small chip ¼" or less	10 to 15%
Chip ¼" to ½"	15 to 20%
Chip ½" to 1"	20 to 25%
Broken piece 1" or larger	25% or more
Multiple broken pieces, but not in in body etching	30% or more
Multiple broken pieces in body etching	50% or more
1" or shorter hairline in body	20 to 35%
1" to 2" hairline in body	25 to 40%
Long hairline or crack in body	30% or more
Short hairline in inlay	15 to 25%
Long hairline in inlay	20 to 30%
Cracks in inlay	30 to 40%
Missing inlay	30 to 40%
Missing base	60% or more
Missing handle	40% or more
Hairline in handle	15 to 25%

These reductions assume that the repairs have been completed and are of high quality. For unrepaired or inadequately repaired pieces a larger reduction would obviously be necessary.

A.11 Repair Costs

While almost any type of damage can be repaired, the cost of repairs can sometimes be higher than the finished product is worth. An approximate range of what you might expect to pay for a high quality repair of various types of damage is as follows. Most repairs should fall into these ranges, but some can be much simpler, or more difficult, than the average repair.

Repair chip	$15 to $40
Repair one broken piece in base	$20 to $70
Repair multiple broken pieces in base	$50 to $100
Repair crack in handle	$30 to $50
Repair multiple cracks in handle	$40 to $80
Repair hairline in inlay	$25 to $50
Repair cracks in inlay	$30 to $70
Repair short hairline in body	$30 to $60
Repair long crack in body	$40 to $100
Repair heavy cracks in body	$75 to $200

It is also possible to have a new inlay or even a new handle or base made for a stein. The finished results can vary from an excellent copy to an obvious replacement, with the following approximate costs.

New inlay	$50 to $75
New handle	$100 to $125
New base	$125 to $175

As a general rule, a new part should be used only if the original part is missing or is beyond repair. A new inlay is generally considered to have the same value as a repaired inlay with heavy damage. A new handle or base is considered to have a lower value than a repaired part. Very few people are capable of making these high quality replacement parts.

Pewter repairs can also be done well by only a handful of people. Because of the difficulty and time-consuming nature of the work, the cost of such repairs can seem quite expensive. Examples of the costs of pewter repairs follow.

Attach new thumblift	$25 to $50
Reattach original thumblift	$15 to $20
Repair crack in pewter	$20 to $40
Repair loose strap	$15 to $25
Replace defective hinge	$40 to $60

While it is generally worthwhile to repair most minor damage on Mettlach steins, it is obvious that repairs of serious damage on lower priced steins should not be considered.

A.12 Print Under Glaze Blanks

Many print under glaze blank steins can be found, particularly with the 1526 and 1909 body styles. These occur both with and without lids. No significant value should be placed on these steins: without lids, ½-liter and 1-liter PUG blanks are worth about $25, with lids they are worth about $50 to $70.

Occasionally a PUG blank will be found to have been painted over with a decoration. If the decoration is partially worn away or very plain, do not attach any additional value to the stein.

Perhaps as many as several hundred different advertising decorations have been applied to PUG blanks, many were done for companies in the United States. Usually very small quantities were made, with values generally running between $125 to $200 for these steins, lower without lids. Brewery or beer-related subjects command the highest prices for these types of steins.

A.13 Unique and Unusual Variations

Major variations from the basic design of a Mettlach stein may be found from time to time. Music box bases are sometimes quite deep (Fig. 36) and can add ½'' or more to the height of a stein. These generally have a nominal influence on the value of the stein. If the music box is present and in working condition, add about $50 to the value of the stein. If the music box is missing add nothing.

Special inscriptions, such as *F.O.E.* on 3135 or *Rip Van Winkle* on 2809, do not influence the value of the stein. These are factory variations that are found fairly often. An inscription etched in or fired onto the body of the stein, made for a specific individual or a one-time purpose, will reduce the stein's value, the extent will depend upon the visual effect of the inscription.

Fig. 36 2230 .5L with music box base and with regular base

Appendix B. Important Information for Collectors

In the years that I have been dealing in Mettlach and other steins, it has become clear that the widespread collecting of Mettlach steins, has begun only quite recently. Rarely have I met or heard of serious collectors who began collecting before about 1955. Today there are probably five times the number of serious Mettlach stein collectors as there were then. A few reasons can be cited for this tremendously increased interest in Mettlach wares. First, a general increase of interest in antiques of all types has taken place, concentrating particularly upon turn-of-the-century items. The remaining reasons are due to the more ready availability of information about Mettlach wares. There has been a realization that it would be impossible to reproduce the beauty and quality of Mettlach items at a competitive price, particularly the etched and cameo wares. Articles and books have frequently promoted the beauty and desirability of these antiques. Finally, there has been a substantial growth of *Stein Collectors International,* a club for the collectors of antique drinking vessels, which although basically a general stein club, has greatly concentrated the interests, knowledge, and ardor of its largest constituency, the Mettlach collectors. It is hoped that this book, with its explanations of manufacturing techniques, variations, and rarities among the Mettlach wares, will also add to the knowledge about these wares and thus to their collectability.

B.1 Original Sources

At the time Mettlach steins and other wares were first made, many of them were exported directly to retail stores in the United States. This probably accounts for the majority of the supply of steins and other wares that are presently in the U.S. In the 1950's large quantities of Mettlach and other steins were brought to the U.S. by antiques importers, although this flow has been reversed in more recent times. Soldiers and tourists from the 1940's to the 1960's also accounted for some of the present inventory in the U.S. Most of these steins that were in houses throughout the country, one here and there, are now in collections. These collections are in the semi-permanent possession of serious collectors, and increasingly in the permanent collections of museums. As the sources have slowly become less fruitful, the prices of desirable pieces have inexorably increased.

B.2 Collection Strategies

Since Mettlach steins and other wares come in many sizes and types, and cover a wide range of prices, different approaches to collecting are possible. Collections always contain certain elements of similarity and certain elements of diversity. I know of only one collector who has concentrated on obtaining many examples of the same stein, and yet his collection is still quite striking. Mostly collections of Mettlach steins are diversified, having examples of PUGs, relief, cameo, and etched steins, although some have concentrated on a specific type. Sizes can be all the same or diversified. Some people concentrate on drinking scenes, comical scenes, or unusual shapes.

Most collectors enjoy the quest of putting together sets or pairs, particularly of the scarcer or more aesthetically pleasing items. The artistic arrangement of a collection can also greatly enhance its appeal to the collector, and the use of plaques, bowls, and other items together with steins provides an additional dimension that ought to be considered.

A collection should contain what the individual collector likes, and not what seems to be in vogue, rare, or expensive. If you like a stein there will always be a proper place for it to be displayed in your collection.

B.3 Investing Versus Collecting

During the 1960's and early 1970's Mettlach wares proved to be a very good investment, both in comparison to other antiques and to other investment possibilities. Their performance in the mid- and late- 1970's was not as strong, with some other antiques increasing in value far more rapidly. In the last two years, with the deflation of many of those antique values, however, Mettlach steins and other Mettlach wares have remained steady and thus have proved to be a relatively strong, if unspectacular, performer.

It is difficult to predict a precise future price trend, but based upon past performance it is likely that Mettlach antiques will be a fairly good investment on a long-term basis. A general and rapid appreciation in prices over any short period of time is unlikely, but there will always be a few spectacular performers. These will be the items that are increasingly popular today but were not popular, and thus not commonly ordered, when they were introduced. Those steins and other wares that were originally relatively expensive are often quite beautiful and yet usually rare, and thus may offer potential for those also interested in the investment angles.

B.4 Original Prices

At the time Mettlach steins were made it was difficult for the average wage earner to afford them. In 1900 the average annual earnings for an American industrial worker was $438, or about 15ᶜ an hour (according to the 1975 *Historical Statistics of the U.S.*). The most popular ½-liter etched Mettlach steins cost between $2 and $3 once transported and displayed for retail sale. Prices were, of course, higher for 1-liter steins, and the larger steins could cost $20 or more. Relief and PUG ½-liter steins sold for about $1.

Examples of retail prices in the U.S. can be found in the E.R. Thieler catalog. At a consistent 23.8ᶜ to the German Mark (1890 to 1910 *Wall Street Journals*) these prices are exactly 2.31 times those in the Villeroy & Boch 1905 catalog, reflecting the markup for transporting and marketing these steins.

Number	Size	Price
675	.5L	$9.24 per dozen
1028	.5L	$11.88 per dozen
1395	.5L	$2.28
1526/1143	.5L	$1.02
1578	4.5L	$14.57
1675	.5L	$2.55
1786	.5L	$3.74
1819	.5L	$2.83
1909/983	.5L	$1.29
1909/1212	.5L	$1.29
1940	3.0L	$7.32
2001	.5L	$2.28
2002	.5L	$2.28
2002	1.0L	$2.75
2090	.3L	$1.95
2090	.5L	$2.28
2090	1.0L	$3.03
2093	.5L	$2.14
2140/1047	.5L	$1.54
2182	.5L	$15.84 per dozen
2205	5.2L	$11.72
2210	3.25L	$3.25
2219	3.15L	$4.57
2261/1012	2.25L	$4.02
2271/1055	.5L	$1.70
2324	.5L	$2.55
2382	.5L	$2.83
2382	1.0L	$4.12
2388	.5L	$1.15
2402	.5L	$2.83

Number	Size	Price
2419/1041	4.15L	$6.33
2455	6.8L	$19.25
2778	.25L	$2.09
2778	.5L	$2.83
2778	1.0L	$3.58
2808	.5L	$2.55
2828	.5L	$3.68
2828	1.0L	$4.67
2833	.3L	$1.70
2833	.5L	$1.87
2936	.5L	$2.55
2956	3.1L	$5.94
3099	3.0L	$6.77
3135	.5L	$2.55
3135 (music box)	.5L	$3.65
Plaque 1044/221		$1.65
Plaque 1044/1206		$2.75
Plaque 2323		$3.85
Plaque 2362		$4.40
Plaque 7037		$5.50
Plaque 7052		$8.25

These prices are roughly consistent with prices in an advertisement by Rothschild Bros. Department Store in Ithaca NY from the 1904 *Cornell Alumni News,* which shows the following.

Number	Size	Price
485	.5L	$1.75
675	.5L	$0.85
1180	.5L	$1.00
1675	.5L	$2.00
2001	.5L	$2.50
2002	.5L	$3.75
2012	.5L	$1.50
2077	.3L	$0.90
2090	.5L	$2.00
2388	.5L	$1.25
2871	1.0L	$4.00
2872	.5L	$2.50

For those who have even greater interest in the original prices they can be found in the book (Thomas, Post, 1975). Within each of the sizes the steins with the highest original prices were generally the etched or glazed steins with unusual shapes or gold decoration.

B.5 Current Price Trends

Many factors contribute to the value of a specific Mettlach stein. The quality of the design, subject matter, workmanship, and condition are some of the more obvious factors. Unlike some assets which have alternative productive uses, steins and other Mettlach items have a value only as something beautiful to collect or to accumulate for enjoyment or speculation. For this reason the value of any Mettlach item is simply what one person will pay another in order to own it; dealers do not and could not collude to set prices.

Values listed in this book are the *retail* prices that a collector can expect to pay when items are in good condition and are being sold by a knowledgeable seller. Factors which could cause a wide discrepancy in the price, such as damage or less desirable lids, have been explained in Appendix A.

From time to time steins or other Mettlach items may be sold by collectors, dealers, or auction houses at substantially higher or lower prices than are shown here. Individual sales at noticeably different prices would not change the value of a Mettlach item. A consistent trend of different prices, however, would tend to alter the retail price, provided that the transactions were by knowledgeable individuals acting without any unusual influences such as a desire to quickly liquidate their assets.

The *wholesale* price of a Mettlach stein can vary a great deal, depending upon the item or items involved, as well as the needs of the buyer. The more desirable steins will tend to have higher wholesale values (relative to their retail prices) than the less desirable steins. While most dealers like to have margins of 40 to 50%, it is realistic to expect to sell a nice quality collection of Mettlach steins to a dealer for about 75% of the retail value. A very high quality collection could receive an even higher percentage because many of these pieces may be quickly placed in waiting collections.

A common error that has been repeated by many authors and collectors is that there can be a wide range in the price of a stein, based upon geography. In fact geography plays little role in determining the value of a stein. Everything else being equal the *selling* price of a stein will be the same in Los Angeles, Boston, Chicago, Houston, Miami, Duluth, Fargo, Butte, or only slightly higher or lower in Munich.

What is the trend of Mettlach stein prices? That is a frequently asked question, and while it is easy to review the change in prices from 1958 to 1983, it is difficult to predict future performance.

In 1956 the average, ½-liter etched stein sold for $20 to $25. Over the next few years increases were modest, but during the 1960's prices increased rapidly until at the start of the 1970's the average ½-liter etched stein sold for $200 to $300, with some higher. By 1975 the most desirable ½-liter steins were approaching $1000, with the majority of the ½-liter etched steins priced between $300 to $500. From 1975 through 1980 prices increased less than 10% per year for most ½-liter etched steins, with increases on some of the more expensive steins being a little greater. With the economic slowdown and the high yields of monetary investments, 1981 and 1982 saw relatively little change in price.

Larger sized etched steins, cameo, and faience steins and plaques have shown about the same trends as the ½-liter etched steins. Print under glaze, relief, mosaic, art nouveau, and tapestry steins experienced slower growth in price during the early 1970's and about the same or higher percentage growth than etched steins in the last 6 or 7 years.

As for the future, the relatively strong performance of Mettlach steins over the past two years, while other antiques have decreased in price, seems to indicate a very solid base. It is the *collectors* that have created the demands and prices for Mettlach wares not the *investors*. This lack of investment money artifically forcing up the price of steins, beyond the price collectors would be willing to pay, has kept the prices firm even as investment opportunities changed drastically. As economic conditions improve and money market rates become less attractive it seems likely that old and new collectors will plunge back into the bidding war with museums and the resultant Mettlach prices will continue upward.

B.6 Locating Steins

Although Mettlach steins and other wares cannot generally be considered to be quite rare, it is true that you will not find them for sale in every antique shop through which you might wander. You have to know where to look. The vast majority of Mettlach steins that are sold each year are sold by a small number of dealers and a few collectors upgrading or disposing of their collections.

If the intent of a collector is to buy a Mettlach stein only occasionally and with little consideration for the type or characteristics of the stein then canvasing the antique shops and antique shows should yield the desired results. However, should a specific objective be important, such as acquiring a nicely planned collection, it would be advantageous to develop contacts with knowledgeable and trustworthy dealers and collectors.

B.7 Protecting Your Collection

First there are some common-sense procedures to follow so as to keep from damaging your own steins. Hot beverages should be kept out of steins, and no hot water washes or dishwashers should be used to clean steins - just use luke warm water, mild soap, and a soft brush. Displaying steins in sunlit windows, or storing them in extremely hot or cold locations, can cause stress lines to develop in the bodies of the steins. Wrapping steins in newspaper and storing them in damp basements can discolor the pewter. When choosing a place to display steins find an area free from flying objects, swinging brooms, or vacuum cleaner handles. Instruct curious friends in the proper techniques for holding or examining steins, warn them especially not to flop closed the inlaid or heavy pewter lids.

Steins occasionally break when transported. Wrap and box them carefully, then wrap and rebox the first box, and insure all packages that are sent.

Finally, valuable collections in homes should be fully covered by insurance policies; and to protect larger collections security systems should also be considered. Stein dealers can provide you with accurate insurance appraisals of your pieces for nominal fees. Do not advertise your home address, use a post office box or work through a dealer.

B.8 Making Worthwhile Purchases

If Mettlach wares are bought at prices near to those in this book, you will be receiving a fair value for your money. These are prices that other collectors are willing to pay for the same pieces. Of course this assumes that any defects that might exist have been detected and properly discounted.

Recognizing repaired defects has gotten to be increasingly difficult. In the last few years the techniques, materials, and experience developed by a few repairmen have resulted in some excellent repairs being performed on some Mettlach steins. These repairs are very difficult for collectors to detect if they have not been trained to do so. Many Mettlach steins have been sold at auctions, by dealers, and by collectors with repairs or damages that were not indicated to the buyer. Some sellers do not know of the repairs or do not feel obligated to point out repairs or damages to prospective buyers, even when they are fully aware of the defects.

Learning how to detect repairs and damage, and to distinguish them from factory flaws, takes time, and the advice and coaching of experienced collectors or dealers can be helpful. In the meantime, relying on the reputation of the individual dealer or collector from whom you make your purchases is essential.

Do not assume that an advertisement of steins for sale, even one carried in a respectable publication such as an antiques periodical, can be relied upon for accuracy. While most dealers and collectors are honest, a lack of knowledge by some, and a tendency for most of the dishonest dealers to gravitate toward advertising, has left knowledgeable buyers with a cautious suspicion toward advertisements. Many advertisers do deliver what is promised, but be certain you can return the stein if you are not satisfied, and do not expect the publication to be of any help should a problem arise.

Auctions are a totally different way to buy. If you have a very good idea what you are doing, and you have time and patience, you might do very well. If you are not well informed or are not patient, watch out, you are the collector for whom they are waiting. Simple rules to remember for auction buying are:

1) most auctioneers know very little or nothing about steins and even less about repairs;

2) auctions that sell *as is* (no description of condition), naturally tend to attract merchandise with defects that sellers would rather not describe;

3) many auctions are not truly auctions, until the price of the item being sold reaches a level above the price that the consignor (owner) is willing to accept, not all items at auction are *protected* this way but many are; and

4) if a buyer's premium exists, usually 10%, remember to add that to your total cost before you make your bids.

Should you decide to buy steins at an auction, try to arrive in plenty of time to thoroughly examine the steins at the preview. Take copious notes on conditions, qualities, and maximum bids you will make, even for items only remotely of interest to you. If possible try to frequent only those auctioneers who knowledgeably indicate damage and sell to the highest bidder without *protected* prices. Generally, only experience or colleagues will tell which auctioneers these are.

B.9 Reproductions

During the period that Mettlach produced etched or *chromolith* steins, there were many other active stein manufacturers, including Simon Peter Gerz, Marzi and Remy, Merkelbach and Wick, Reinhold-Merkelbach, J.W. Remy, Albert Jacob Thewalt, Matthias Girmscheid, and Hauber and Reuther (HR), all of whom made similar steins. Without a doubt, however, the quality of these steins is not comparable to that of Mettlach steins; the actual production processes and the resultant steins differ significantly. HR and Marzi Remy generally made the best and most attractive imitations of the Mettlach-style etched steins.

It is helpful to note that only Matthias Girmscheid made a stein with a mark that could remotely be confused with a Mettlach trademark. They used a house similar to the *old tower,* with the word *Germany* in a banner below it.

In recent years both the Thewalt Company and Villeroy and Boch have been making steins which somewhat resemble the antique Mettlach etched steins. The general style of the Thewalt steins is similar to the original Mettlach steins, both in general shapes as well as in the designs of the handles, bands, and lids. These steins, however, are not nearly of the quality of the original Mettlach steins and they are clearly marked as being made by Thewalt.

The currently produced Mettlach steins also have the same general shapes and appearances as the antique etched Mettlach steins, but again the similarity ends there. While descriptive literature from the company has varied from indicating that they have reproduced the original workmanship of the *chromolith* process, to claims of simply having been hand painted, even a quick examination reveals a noticeably different product than the original etched steins. The decoration, or scenes, appear to be a transfer or print under glaze type of process that uses paints, opaque colored glazes, or a small quantity of colored slip, giving some additional depth to the colors not possible with a normal PUG transfer. The imitation etching is not of the fine quality as that on the original etched steins and appears to be a final stage of the transfer application sequence. The handle and bands seem to be hand painted. Viewed next to the antique PUG steins the new Mettlach steins compare favorably (and cost almost as much), but viewed next to the antique etched steins the current production compares unfavorably. The bases of these newly created steins clearly show the years they were made.

There are some new porcelain steins with lithophanes on the market, marked *Mattlack* or other perhaps legally motivated misspellings or *Mettlach*. They do not resemble original Mettlach steins in any way.

B.10 Selling

Mettlach steins and other Mettlach items have always had a fairly high degree of liquidity relative to other antiques. Collectors throughout the country are always looking for desirable items to add to their collections. Many antique dealers around the country are also quite anxious to own a Mettlach stein or two, in order to dress up their inventory.

Still it is important to select the proper method, among the many available, for selling your stein or your collection. First there are several avenues open for selling a small number of steins with a fairly low total dollar value.

1) *Direct to a collector:* This is excellent idea, if you know a collector who wants the stein(s) that you want to sell.

2) *To a local antique dealer:* This is fairly easy and appropriate method if a local dealer is willing to pay a fair price for your steins. Keep in mind he has to resell them at a profit. Depending on his location, he may be able to sell them quickly, or he might have to wait a long time before buyers come along. These factors will contribute to the price he can afford to pay. Many dealers will rather take expensive steins on consignment; if they sell then you will get a percentage of the sale price.

3) *Through an auction:* Many auctioneers are anxious to have a Mettlach stein to sell. Expect to pay about a 20% commission, perhaps higher. If a buyer's premium is charged, consider that part of the commission, because the buyer will keep this in mind and bid lower. Rarely do Mettlach steins sell at very high prices at auction, generally they will bring less than the *retail* price.

4) *Advertise in an antiques publication:* Fairly good results can be achieved sometimes, but there is no guarantee the right person will see your advertisement.

5) *Respond to an advertisement from a collector or a dealer in an antiques publication:* Responding to a *want* advertisement from a collector may result in a sale, but he will have to want the stein(s) you are selling in order to pay a fair

price. A dealer who specializes in steins will generally pay a fair wholesale price. He will usually buy for resale at a fairly small margin because his turnover is probably more rapid than the average dealer and he will know steins very well and thus will not have to make allowances to cover his risks due to his ignorance.

Should you have a large collection to sell, realizing a high percentage of the retail price could be of significant importance. A ten percent difference in the total price can amount to a large sum of money. A number of things must be considered. Do you want to sell everything in one group, to one buyer? Do you want to sell immediately, or over a short or perhaps long period of time? Are you willing to work hard at selling your collection; communicating widely, wrapping packages, mailing the steins, and so on. To sell a large collection at retail, you would have to be prepared to undertake the expenses and do the work of being the dealer, advertiser, traveler, wrapper, and shipper. While this is possible, it is not practical for everyone. I have seen some collectors do this successfully, but most that have tried eventually become frustrated and impatient, and ultimately would have faired better with another approach.

A dealer specializing in steins, who is thus familiar with the market, can generally realize a retail price on a greater number of steins from a large collection, and with greater ease, than can a collector selling for the first time. Depending upon the *quality* of the collection, that is to say its desirability, diversification, and condition, a collector can expect to sell a collection to a stein dealer at a discount in the vicinity of 20 to 25% from the retail prices. This can, of course, be altered greatly depending upon the collection and general business factors.

Just as for the small collections, auctions offer a method for disposing of a large collection. Auctions provide a number of options, but certain factors do not vary substantially. It will cost about 20%, frequently higher, to sell a collection at auction. The commission is a percentage of the *selling* price, not the *retail* price. While some steins may perhaps sell at auction above a fair retail price, I have never seen or heard of a large collection that was sold at auction that, on average, achieved a fair retail price. Generally, a collection would do very well to achieve a selling price at auction as close as 5 to 10% of the total retail price. I have also seen and heard of collections that did not get within 40% of the total retail price. While it might be possible to place a minimum selling price on some of the steins, you may have to pay a commission if they do not sell.

This should provide the seller with some ways of calculating the range of prices that are likely to be realized in the sale of Mettlach items. Take these prices, adjust for commissions and buyer's premiums, and compare the results for the various methods of selling. Steins can represent a substantial investment of a seller's time and resources, and it will be well worthwhile for him to take the time to work enough of the mathematics to allow for a good bottom line comparison of these alternative ways of selling a collection.

Glossary

Art nouveau, literally *modern style,* the name of a type of *etched* Mettlach ware that used the bold and flat, art nouveau style of sinuous motifs abstractly based upon seaweed and other plant forms; this style was popular from 1895-1915 and was a rebellion against the derivative style of *historicism.*

Bavaria, a type of Mettlach ware that was marked with the Bavaria *Old Tower trademark;* it was usually grey bodied with a simple *hand-painted design.*

Beaker, a cup-like drinking vessel, sometimes with a handle but never with a lid; Mettlach beakers were almost always .25 liter.

Biedermeier, a *peasant style* of art that was important from 1810-1850, a provincial, rustic, sturdy functionalism favored by the new middle class; this style dictated the design and type of early Mettlach products, which were therefore primarily simplistic and functional tablewares; compare with *historicism.*

Cameo, the name of a type of Mettlach ware that has figures or designs standing out in a very low relief; the relief was made from a translucent, porcelain-like material which allows for contrasting background colors to show through the thinnest areas; compare with *relief* and *phanolith.*

Castle trademark, see *Old Tower trademark.*

Character stein, a stein with a shape designed to represent an object, person, or an animal; Mettlach made only a few character steins, most in the form of animals or apples, and even fewer character beakers.

Chromolith, literally meaning *colored stone,* see *etched.*

Clay slip, an opaque paint-like substance that is made by combining coloring agents and water-thinned clay; it is known that at least 30 different colors of clay slips were used at Mettlach.

Conical lid, a ceramic *inlay* lid usually in the shape of a tiled turret roof.

Crack, an open break; compare with *hairline.*

Decoration number, a number that identifies the design of a decoration, especially on PUG, faience, Delft, and Rookwood items; as opposed to *form number.*

Delft, a type of Mettlach ware that was intended to resemble antique Dutch Delftware; it was made like the Mettlach *faience* wares except that the blue and white colors and the decorative devices are clearly of the Delft style.

Dwarfs, small real people; the so-called dwarfs that are common themes of Mettlach decorations are technically the ageless, tiny, *gnomes* from folklore; does this make dwarf a mis-gnomer?

Etched, the name commonly given to a type of Mettlach ware that uses colored clays or colored *clay slips* to form a smooth matte-finished decoration; this decoration was probably applied from the inside, with a distinctive incised black outlining of uniformly colored areas; see *inlaid* and *reverse painting* theories, and contrast with *glazed.*

Etruscan, in the artistic style of ancient Truscany, which used profiles, no perspective, and colors dominated by shades of brown, tan, black, and creamy white; several etched Mettlach items were made in this style.

Faience, the name of a type of Mettlach ware that was primarily *hand painted;* intended to resemble the 17th and 18th Century German faience-decorated earthenware first made in Faenza, Italy.

Footring, a pewter collar around the base of steins to protect them against chipping and wear; on Mettlach steins they are rarely found on other than faience types.

Form number, or stock number, the number used to identify the mold from which an item was made; compare with *decoration number.*

Four F, or *4F,* a symbol of the German gymnastic or athletic society; the Fs are flipped in a pattern that puts all their corners together making a cross shape; 4F stands for *Frisch, Fromm, Froh, Frei* meaning alert, devout, joyful, free.

Gambrinus, legendary king of Flanders who supposedly discovered beer; he is a subject on many Mettlach decorations.

Glaze, a clear hard ceramic material that was painted onto a stoneware body then fired so as to create a glass-like shiny coating; at Mettlach it is known that they utilized various matte and glossy clear glazes, as well as at least 176 colored hard glazes and 150 colors meant to go under clear glazes.

Glazed, the name of a type of Mettlach ware in which colored *glazes* were painted on from the outside of the product in order to add color to the design; contrast with *etched.*

Gnomes, the ageless, tiny characters from folklore, see *dwarfs.*

Hairline, a closed break that sometimes shows up as a thin black line in stoneware; compare with *crack.*

Hand painted, a type of Mettlach ware that used a blank body and then was either painted and fired, or just cold painted, with some design.

Hein, M., an artist who lived near Mettlach and designed Mettlach wares that ranged from the simpler *mosaic* pieces to the large full color relief steins with buildings on the lids.

Historicism, the style of art that dominated the Continent, including Mettlach styles, from about 1840-1910; it sought a return to the Renaissance with powerful sculptural forms, complicated outlines and friezes, and deep reliefs or contrasting shadows; it originated with archeological findings of numerous awe-inspiring Renaissance artifacts, and in response art schools began instructing pupils by having them copy the forms and ornaments of these artifacts; compare with *Biedermeier* and *art nouveau.*

Incised, refers to lines impressed into the unfired stoneware by means of a stamp, press, or mold; sometimes used synonymously with *etched.*

Inlaid, a theory that proposes that the colored clays or clay slips used in the production of *etched* Mettlach wares were applied from the outside; contrast with *reverse painting.*

Inlay, the name of a type of lid for steins that have a decorated ceramic disk inserted in the pewter flange of the lid.

Jeweled base, a rounded bowl-shaped base having a brown glazed background with friezes and colorfully glazed, simulated cabochon jewels.

Liter, or *L,* the metric measure of capacity, slightly more (1.057) than a quart.

Mercury trademark, a stamped emblem, usually green, that includes the winged head of Mercury, two snake-entwined staffs, a banner inscribed *Villeroy & Boch,* the location of the V&B factory, here *Mettlach,* and at the bottom various semicircles, scalloping, and dots.

Mettlach, village next to the Saar River in West Germany where Villeroy & Boch had one of their ceramic factories; commonly also used as the name of the wares from that factory.

Mosaic, the name of a type of *glazed* Mettlach ware on which colored glazes are painted into protruding, ridged sections of the stoneware.

Munich Child, Munich Maid, or *Munich Monk,* a common theme on Mettlach wares, the symbol of the city of Munich, supposedly showing a monk's robe on the first child born in Munich after the 10th Century massacre.

Occupational stein, a stein with a decoration or shape that depicts or symbolizes an occupation, probably the occupation of the original owner of the stein; Mettlach made a number of occupational steins including series using etched, glazed, PUG, and other styles.

Old Tower trademark, usually an incised mark featuring the famous 10th Century church of the Abbey of Mettlach, below is usually a banner with Mettlach and VB incorporated into its design.

Percent mark, %, a mark occasionally found on Mettlach wares that probably indicates an item has passed a random inspection or sample testing.

Pewter, a very workable metallic alloy containing as much as 90% or more tin with the remainder made up of lead, copper, zinc, bismuth, or antimony; the pewter on Mettlach wares was guaranteed to be free of all lead, which reduces the chance for pitting or scaling of the pewter and makes these wares acceptable for holding food and drink.

Pewter mountings, includes the *footring* and all the pewterwork that is used to attach the lid to the handle of a stein; the attaching pewterwork has a whole set of terminology that is important in describing damage and repairs: the *strap* encircles the handle and a, usually triangular, *strap support* runs somewhat down the outside of the handle; the *shank* goes from the strap to the *hinge;* a *hinge pin* will show on most steins made after about 1860, it will not show on earlier steins; an odd number of *rings* or *teeth* make up the hinge; the *tang* proceeds from the hinge to the *lid rim;* the *thumblift* can be over the hinge or fastened to the rim; if there is an *inlay* a pewter *flange* will hold it in place; the top of some all-pewter lids may contain an ornate pewter *finial.*

Phanolith, or literally *fancy* or *transparent stone,* the name of a type of Mettlach ware that is possibly identical to the *cameo* ware except the relief materials and the process itself may be of finer quality; its *form numbers* are exclusively in the 7000's.

Plaque, a relatively flat decorative wall hanging, those from Mettlach are usually round or rectangular but occasionally other shapes are found.

Pokal, or brimmer, a large, ceremonial, handleless *beaker* with a separate cover and usually a pedestal base.

Porcelain, a rare material among Mettlach wares, made from a fine white clay, quartz, and feldspar; it is hard, glossy, and relatively thin compared to *stoneware.*

Print under glaze, or *PUG,* the name of a type of Mettlach ware that had decal-like or transfer printed decorations, probably made from copper plates and transferred onto a glazed blank ware and protected with another clear hard glaze.

Probe, or *P,* a mark found on Mettlach trial or test-pieces.

PUG, see *Print under glaze.*

Quidenus, Fritz, an artist from Munich who was often employed by Mettlach to design etched decorations of legends, sports, occupations, and other carefully constructed scenes.

Regimental stein, reservist's stein, or *military stein,* a stein that was purchased as a souvenir of the service in the Imperial German Armies, generally dated between 1890 and 1914; the Mettlach versions were PUG steins that used the 2140 blank body.

Relief, the name of a type of Mettlach ware that has figures or designs of opaque material, usually white or tan, that stand out substantially from the smooth or textured background; similar in appearance to the Wedgewood wares; compare with *cameo.*

Reverse painting, a theory that proposes that colored *clay slips* used in the decoration of *etched* wares were applied from the inside or back of the pattern; contrast with *inlaid.*

Rookwood, the name of a type of Mettlach ware decorated with hand painting or spraying, resembling the wares of the Rookwood factory in Ohio with its rich brown background; Rookwood items have *decoration numbers* in the 6000's.

Saint Florian, patron saint of Upper Austria, protector against fire; a subject of a couple common Mettlach steins.

Saint Hubert, according to legend he was converted by the sight of a stag with luminous cross on its head, patron saint of hunters; a subject of the decorations on several Mettlach items.

Schlitt, Heinrich, an artist from Munich who was one of Mettlach's most prolific designers; he specialized in humorous and fantastic scenes for etched and PUG items; he was a freelance artist who is also well known for his murals, illustrations, and occasional oil paintings.

Schultz, W., an artist from Hanau who designed some of the finest etched steins and plaques; he used allegorical styles with scrolls, ornate borders, and other decorative devices so typical of the style of *historicism.*

Stahl, Johann Baptist, an important so-called modeler at Mettlach; starting in about 1895 he designed many of the cameo and phanolith wares.

Stein, literally meaning *stone,* is probably a shortened form of *Steinzeugkruge,* or *stoneware tankard;* a drinking vessel with a handle and an attached lid, sometimes similar vessels without lids are still called steins.

Stein Collectors International, or *S.C.I.,* a club for the collectors of antique drinking vessels, concentrating mainly on steins; membership, which includes a subscription to the quarterly publication *Prosit,* can be gotten by sending the current annual dues of $20 to S.C.I., P.O. Box 463, Kingston, NJ 08528.

Stoneware, a vitrified ceramic material, usually a silicate clay, that is very hard, rather heavy, and impervious to liquids and most stains.

Stuck, Prof. Franz von, an artist from Munich who designed several etched steins for Mettlach.

Tapestry, the name of a type of *etched* Mettlach ware on which the colorful design is all contained on a tapestry-like front panel.

Transfer printing, see *print under glaze.*

Warth, Christian, an artist who came to Mettlach in 1854 and later became the director of the art department; he may have designed a substantial number of relief items, but his name only appears on a number of later etched designs that generally include knights, students, city views, and common scenes.

(2140) .5L, no decoration
number, the Mettlach
hospital stein Christmas 1917

Index of Illustrations

The first section lists the form numbers of Mettlach wares illustrated in this book. The later section lists the decoration number of PUG wares that are illustrated.